AT HOME, AWAY FROM HOME

(A MEMOIR)

by

TANURE OJAIDE

AT HOME, AWAY FROM HOME
Copyright © Tanure Ojaide, 2017
All rights reserved

ISBN: 978-0-9978689-8-2

Published by:

CISSUS WORLD PRESS
P.O. Box 240865,
Milwaukee, WI 53224
www.cissusworldpressbooks.com

Distributor:

African Books Collective
www.africanbookscollective.com
orders@africanbookscollective.com

Cover Art: Dr. Bruce Onobrakpeya

1

SELF-INTRODUCTION

Nobody wants to be a stranger at home, even if one wants to feel at home in an alien country. I have multiple homes. I may be one of those folks practicing place polygamy in this age of globalization. I feel at home in the United States but not all the time. I have another home, Nigeria, where I also have many homes. The longing to go or visit my natal home often seizes me, as if possessed by the god of nativity, and then to my home country I go. At the same time, sometimes I feel like leaving my original home for an alien place which is now also my home. And so I am drawn both ways, in a tough tug of war, depending upon where I find myself—I am caught up in an unending oscillation; now at home and wishing to leave, and soon outside and wishing to be back at home. Often I feel I am a stranger no matter how long I have lived and worked in the United States. Even if I don't want to see myself as a stranger, others continue to see me as such from their responses to me. Maybe I have perpetuated that perception through my actions and behavior. I have refused to blend, it seems. I refused to be a penguin among penguins and stubbornly chose to remain a pelican. In a world of catfish, I have refused to wear whiskers. I wear materials that make me stand out as an outsider, an African, a Nigerian, a foreigner. I speak English with an African accent. Though some Americans flatter me by saying they love my singsong accent, others are not patient enough to listen to what is not a Southern accent of the American language or any other accent they are familiar with. There are other differences of beliefs and ideas where I hold to mine and do not follow the mainstream. We seem to see things often from different perspectives, with me as a postcolonial fellow, so to say, and the others from their metropolitan position of power. I know I was already formed as a man before my relocation. Maybe I am what I am by choice or remain so instinctively.

I introduce myself as a Nigerian writer teaching at the University of North Carolina at Charlotte. I remember some years back at Durham in my state of North Carolina, the director of the State's Arts Council and her board wondered why I had stayed in North Carolina for so long and yet didn't write about my experience in it. I write about my experience in North Carolina but it is admittedly minuscule or rather minimal in my overall writings. Is it because I don't want to write about it or the inspiration to write about it doesn't just come? The inspiration to write about experiences set in Nigeria seems to come effortlessly and naturally. It is difficult to forget where one grew up, I have come to realize. A writer's (perhaps everybody's) childhood and youth cannot be shed easily. Mine stick to me as if I have been so immersed in them as for them to be inseparable from me. I am a transplant of the Niger Delta and it seems I cannot shed my nativity wherever I find myself. I am so suffused in the elements of the Niger Delta that we appear to be one. Whatever other soil nourishes me gets absorbed into this self, which was already formed before I left home. That is, however limited the village of my childhood and youth might look in a global perspective, the experiences there remain impinging on my daily life as an adult.

Surprisingly, despite the comfort and cosmopolitanism of the new home in the United States, with me middle aged and now older, the earlier experiences overwhelm my new ones! My childhood and youth are most indelible for their sense of adventure, happiness, richness, and a plethora of experiences that make me always yearn for them. One does not forget what one yearns for at heart. That desire to relive the old days can never be erased by new experiences, however one feels. In my case, it is the result of my childhood and youth days that brought me to the United States. I was formed before I left home and cannot be changed much, however flexible I want to be. Already rooted in the Niger Delta with its then fresh air, food, and water, the transplant has adjusted so well that irrespective of the new climate and soil, it retains the properties of its native self. After all, long ago before globalization became a fad, I had concluded that it no longer mattered where you lived! That is, if you are already properly formed and whole, you can survive anywhere else you choose to live. I know I have come to live in America by chance and instead of being here I might as well be living in England, Zimbabwe, Nigeria, or elsewhere. That is, if I found a sabbatical job in those places when I was looking for one when at the University of Maiduguri in 1988, I might be living in any of those places. Whitman College, Walla Walla, Washington State, gave me the break in a streak of rejections and silences from Nigerian universities and an unattractive offer from the University of London, and that brought me to the United States.

So the cherry fruits, breadfruits, wild apples, mangoes, grapes, and avocadoes of my childhood still torment me with their savage freshness and taste. I have the same feeling for the freshwater fish, most of them no longer in the waters of the creeks and streams that Shell and other multinational oil corporations have literally shat chemicals into. Where are the *okpogu* and *omwa* fish with their spikes or swords? Where is the *orhirhi*, the jelly and electric fish? Where is the *ogbene*, the snake fish whose length and head will still instill fear of a real snake in me? Where is the *urhirhie*, that long miniature of the catfish? Where are these unique fishes and a host of others that were so tasty in Grandma's soup pot? Why will I not be drawn to go back to where in thunderstorms fish fell from the sky, as the elders told young ones? There was an armada or flotilla of *ikere*, a black Pygmy breed of frogs, swamping the deluged land? What will stop me from yearning for days when the electric or jelly fish and mudfish lived in holes in dry

4

streams and creeks till the next raining season when they were liberated from their dungeon of mud?

The landscape of my childhood and youth is littered with anthills, mushrooms, water leaf, as well as different species of palm trees, irokos, obeches, and other flora. The forest shone with luster in a green canopy that shielded one from the hot strokes of the archer sun. Creeks crisscrossed the landscape and the farms were often guarded by an army of butterflies. Different fruit plants were in the forests and one could spend a whole day replenished by the natural resources that made the bush also a home of sorts to non-human beings.

There are some things that cannot be held back, and the resources of my childhood and youth days are among such things. I love water but the creeks and streams where we went to pick flying fish and literally use a machete to cut fish in shallow creeks at night have been clogged mainly by the oil companies' negligence resulting in oil spills and my people's inability to refurbish the water home of their goddess, Mami Wata. Still, I cannot resist the pull to go to the home of my youth. There is a mystical attraction for me to the soil where my umbilical cord was buried. Pity it was not kept and frozen in a lab for stem cell research to cure currently incurable diseases or conditions. I am sure my family and I would have benefitted from such research to make us far healthier than we are now. But wherever it is in the village that no longer exists in the forests, even if the umbilical cord dissolved into the soil, it is part of me living underground somewhere that pulls me to walk on.

And that's despite the inadequacy of modern amenities in the home place after being pampered by a developed country's lifestyle. But happiness is not necessarily tied to development. I don't know whether or not it was because of childhood or youth, I carried happiness effortlessly in Ibada Village, where I was born to be raised by my Grandmother. Grandma Amreghe treated me to the delights of the village.

5

Ibada Village does not appear in any map I know of but it remains indelible in my memory. This village of Okpara in today's Delta State no longer exists because it was abandoned for Okurekpo by the roadside but it remains fresh and thriving in my memory.

Of course, many nowadays would scare you about the lack of electric light for the one hundred and eighty million people, the extremely bad roads, brainless drivers, and diseases that were on the prowl to seize upon anyone from abroad who has lost his or her immunity. There are many scare tactics out there to exaggerate the shortcomings of the Niger Delta. The feeble heart would seize upon the excuses of those who don't know the place and stay back in the luxury of a developed country and forget about their other home. Such folks forget about where they were born; they also forget about where they lived as children and youths. They would forget so much as to forget about themselves. But I believe the waters of the creeks will not forget their boatman as long as they remain pliable. The soil of the Niger Delta will not forget the soles of the homeboy who only knew about shoes during Christmas and New Year period in his later childhood. The air of the rainforest will always be ally to the homeboy whose lungs it has strengthened with clean and fresh draughts. I am one of theirs.

And so I prepared to leave my American home to go to my Niger Delta home. To go there and experience my heart's desire. Go to my real home and be one with my early providers whom I still credit with my wellbeing. Go home and taste what nourished me all the years to make me what I am before others recognized me for what I am. I looked forward to going home. I had been a captive of the spirit of migration and I sought liberation. Going home would bring me freedom that I sought and looked forward to relishing. When one travels, one prays for a safe return. One goes to the market and returns; one goes out to fish or hunt and returns home.

To go home, I had to seek a fellowship, if I wanted to stay for a full year or more as I wanted. I could only do as much with a small grant from the university. Maybe enough funds to stay for six weeks at most but not a full year. I had stayed at home for two weeks, four weeks, and even six weeks. I had thought I was current with Nigerian issues and knew the Nigerian experience. But I wanted a longer stay to fully know my home. The opportunity came when I received a Fulbright fellowship to teach in a Nigerian university and also to study the folklore of my people with particular attention to *udje* as an oral poetic performance. But I did not anticipate what one full year would do to me. I did not expect to be overwhelmed with a deluge of knowledge that could sweep one away into a sea of delirium.

One can stare at so much and not know what things stare back at one. The same applies to human beings. I had a full year of knowledge that has made me to feel that I did not know my country, I did not know my people, I did not know much for all the years I lived there before I came to the United States. A gap that has become a gaping hole stood between me and my homeland. It was a full year that was an eye-opener. It would appear that I had been staring at things without seeing them; I had been listening without hearing. I would see and hear so much that had escaped my watchful eyes and attentive ears. I had to cross the ocean many times to see and hear properly. I would retouch things for a new experience. I would smell things too and come away with a new sensation. I was going to live with spirits because my home has transformed into a land of spirits that God's medicine men and pastors would use different rites to try to exorcise without success. I was going to live in the belly of a beast that had possessed an entire country. It needed a miracle in the country of believers fighting against poverty, demonic grip, and a host of adversities to come out safe and whole.

Of course, as a writer, I expected to be inspired to write poems and short stories. After all, my muse, Aridon, has always been native to my home too. Aridon has followed me wherever I went or lived. Now Aridon, my muse, invites me home for a feast that I believe no doubt will be exhilarating. After all, my muse belongs to a class of her own. In her I always discern a unique energy, which properly harnessed, would result in strong and illuminating creative works. From my experience as a poet, I know that whatever happened in this trip home and at home, the new space and all its institutions and characters would fetch me songs and narratives that would be testaments to my one year "at home, away from home."

Ibada Village

The village dropped out of existence but didn't die.
For sure Ibada Village didn't die from abandonment.

True, I cannot wander in the abandoned landscape;
I cannot greet dead residents with a child's voice—

no one catches me from the back; mock kidnaping
that today is a real threat to freedom of movement.

Today no oldies walking spritely proffering advice
from their calabash of wisdom that's never exhausted;

yes, no parent still buries the umbilical cord outside
with stem cell research needing it for vital research;

no garden of kola nuts or pepper fruits to welcome visitors;
everyone's no longer a farmer or gardener self-sustaining.

The village has no ghosts but innumerable shadows.

I see the dead and those transformed into new figures.

Ibada dropped out of existence to allow Okurekpo grow.
Folks abandoned village paths for macadamized roads.

Today the town-crier walks no town of mine,
the town peopled with houses standing apart.

I live in the abandoned village throbbing and not
in my city residence without the village beauty.

Ibada thrives not with industries, not with traffic
but for sure the abandoned village didn't die.

2

IN MY FATHER'S HOUSE

I was to be booked to fly to Abuja through Europe but I opted to fly to Lagos directly from the United States. It was for a purpose that I wanted my international flight to stop in Lagos even though I would have to get to Abuja from there on my own. I wanted to go to the Delta first, experience the place before going anywhere else in Nigeria. The morning following my arrival in Lagos, I took a Sienna minivan to Effurun, one of my homes in Nigeria. It was from this base that I began exploring my native home.

I am my father's first-born son. I am the *owaran*, the family priest of the Dafetanure Ojaide line. Can I, named Moses on the first day in elementary school, be an effective family priest? My family vocation of priesthood might have been corrupted and compromised right from when very young from being a proper traditional family counsellor, family priest, and family head. That was from the time I was given Moses as my name on my first day at elementary school by a teacher who insisted I needed another name other than the one my parents gave me. By another name, the teacher meant a Christian or European name. My parents were not consulted and I considered that name foreign and not mine. Are any folks in England called Emoghware or Tanure? Do foreigners name British children for them? Much as Moses would appeal to those whose culture has the name, it is not an Urhobo name. I would shed the name later in life to be a proper first-born of my father. Today, only very few, who knew me as Moses in my early youth, call me by that name.

I did not live in my father's village. I was not even born there. I was born and raised in my mother's village of Ibada under the tutelage of my Grandmother, the irrepressible

Mother Hen, Amreghe, to whom I owe so much. As first-born son, I have to clean my father's grave and take proper care of it. Seniority from the womb comes with responsibilities, and I did not need to be told. One knew one's place once one finds oneself in that place. I had rebuilt my father's house after his death. I had a plan to build a house for him at Okpara Inland, the main town from which many villages sprang from, including Enemarho. We had planned that he would move there after the completion of the more modern house, but death did not obey human wishes and plans. Death does not wait for people to fulfill their goals of where to live or when to leave one place to another for permanent settlement. And so, despite the sand packed there, despite many cement blocks already molded for the bungalow, my father died before the execution of the plan. And so he had to be buried in the Enemarho Village, where he had always lived. He had been born there but not in the compound in which he died. He had moved from what had been described as the old village to the new village, from deeper in the bush to the roadside of the Okurekpo-Samagidi Road.

I had not visited there for over twenty years. I had sent money for the house to be rebuilt. The old house with mud walls and corrugated iron roof had to be made modern—cement block walls and new roofs. I had asked a friend of mine rather than my brothers or other family relatives to do the work. Of course, there were many complaints. "Have you seen the house your boy is helping you to build?" they would phone me. They called him "boy" even though he had become an Associate Professor and soon a Full Professor. "Will a strong storm not blow the house down?" they complained. "Look at the type of doors he has installed. The house is not properly built." They were not builders but they complained because I did not give them the assignment, which should have been an easy way of spending my money without accounting for it. If they had built the house, they would keep part of my money to do a major project for themselves. I did not trust them for much of the work but later buckled and sent money to one brother to do some things. He got the money for the same job several times and nothing was done. His junior asked why he was not being engaged to do anything in the house project. "The carpentry work is too shoddy and many things need to be redone," he told me. I wired him some money and nothing was done. I waited for a long time to receive a report of what had been done. No report came to me. The money had gone down the drains. At last my friend completed the house and by then my relatives, who did not do anything substantial with the money I had sent them, kept quiet.

So, for my visit to my father's house, I had to go and see the house I had asked to be built and had not seen since its completion for more than fifteen years. A first cousin had challenged me whether I had seen the house I had asked to be built. He wanted me to be coming home to where he had migrated from to the city. He no longer lived there but went there the third Sunday of every other month for a family meeting. So, there is where the extended Ojaide family holds its bi-monthly meetings. They discuss family issues and how to bring together the large family as a coherent unit. I have never attended any of the meetings and so have given them enough cause to complain about me. They complain that they don't see me, as if they want me to fly from the United States to Enemarho Village for the bi-monthly extended Ojaide family meeting. The meeting holds in the sitting room of my father's house that I had sent money to be rebuilt. The family, through my cousin I had helped his son to come to Atlanta, Georgia, to study Fine Arts, asked me to buy one hundred plastic chairs to sit them at the meeting. I knew they were not up to one hundred by any count but wanted me to send money for them to use for some other things. Later my cousin who could reach me by phone said they would rent out the chairs to those having parties or gatherings in the neighborhood. I knew they wanted to make money out of me by renting chairs to those doing weddings and burial ceremonies, the two most important and regular parties in Urhobo land every weekend. I bought fifty plastic chairs to quieten them.

Once I decided to visit my father's house, I invited my friend, Dr. Jonathan, to accompany me. To Dr. Jonathan, I am the brother he never had. To me, he is the senior brother I didn't have. He drove to me in Effurun and we took off in my Toyota 4-Runner for Okurekpo to pick my mother and Erhire, my surviving brother, for the trip to Enemarho Village.

It is not easy to be a first-born male in the family among my people, it appears. An old friend of mine, whom I call Barrister, told me that he could not point a finger at a firstborn male doing well, especially from our traditional polygamous society in Agbon. I felt happy and scared at the same time because of the observation. I felt happy that though firstborn and male, I consider myself lucky to be happy with myself and my own family. Of course, I was scared because the firstborn male is often at a great risk in his extended family. Barrister explained the traditional culture to me. The firstborn male is targeted by his mother's co-wives so as not to inherit much of what the father leaves behind. The firstborn also faces the attacks of his father's family members on inheritance and land issues. Land has always been a cause of conflict not only between families but also within a family. In the patriarchal system, the senior son takes over from his father and that is an envied position in the man's household and in his extended family. The firstborn son's elimination or weakness would be a boon to the family members that would appropriate his father's lands, plantations, and streams to their own. Greed is a major feature of the genetic makeup of my people. But the plight of the firstborn male remains troubling to me.

It brought memories of my last paternal uncle to die to my mind. Oroyovwe, which means "for whom things are well" when the name is translated literally, styled himself *Owhorode*, a big man, a very important person, but he was poor. A penny would down him, as our people would describe his wretchedness. Later in life, he joined a club of big people and so he saw himself as a big man. The club of big people did not seem to have changed his fate. Penury would not let him out of its grip. He was a beggar despite his self-styled importance. On one of my rare visits, after greeting him and doing what I should for an ageing uncle, he sat me down in his vast but disheveled sitting room. There was something he had always wanted to tell me since my father died, he said. Or more, a remark he wanted to make about my father, his own senior brother.

"Your father was very cunning. He was a tortoise among us. He kept it a secret for four years that you were a girl and not a boy!"

"I didn't know that," I told him.

"He was cleverer than Orose, the tortoise," he said.

"God bless him!" I told myself.

I got the meaning of what my uncle said. I was a deer and you don't have to explain what the forest is to it. But I wondered that none of my father's people, uncles, aunts, and an array of relatives, did not care to come to my mother's village to say hello to the newborn even though described as a girl. Even a girl is a human being that should be loved and bonded with. But their oversight, by his interpretation of events, was my good luck. Yes, very good luck seemingly saved me, according to what I could infer from my uncle's frank talk with me.

During this one year at home after being away for so long except for occasional short visits, I reached out to perhaps the only childhood friend I had from my father's village. Though I did not live there, somehow we were close as young men. Dennis was not an Ojaide. Dennis Onakpoma and I were age-mates and that fact must have made us very close whenever we met outside Enemarho Village. We talked on the phone several times before I went to visit him in Sapele. He entertained me very warmly and I felt happy meeting him. There is a certain unique feeling of nostalgia on meeting an old childhood friend who remains cheerful whenever you are together. In a sober moment, he told me what I had never thought about.

"If you were born and raised in our village, you wouldn't be what you are today."

"You mean with respect to education?" I asked.

"Education and all," he replied.

The idea sank in. I was from a polygamous household. My father had a daughter from a woman I did not see. Ledi was married and lived in a Kokori village. By the time I was growing up in Ibada Village, my father had another wife from Kokori. Could one not do well in a polygamous family if a firstborn male? I silently asked myself. In any case, if it was a trap, I had already escaped it. But Dennis had reminded me of the mysteries and complexities I was not exposed to as a child, since I lived with my maternal grandmother. Of course, I would have had no Mother Hen in my father's compound even though my mother was there. I was given to Grandmother Amreghe, she always insisted, to protect and she would have put her life many times down to defend me. I did not think of safety as a child but there was one who took it as her divine duty to protect a baby and nourish him to a strong boy and man. That was the great Mother Hen, Amreghe.

I recalled what happened during my father's burial in December 1985. Many relatives of the extended family came around to support me in the ceremony. My senior first cousin, Raleigh, most likely born the year the first Raleigh bicycle came to the village, was in attendance. He had been away for as long as I could remember. He had been farming in Ekiadolor, near Benin. If only hard work made anyone prosperous, he would be very prosperous. But he was not yet prosperous at the time. He must be resentful of the extended family from his remarks.

"If you have universal family approval, you think you would not have advanced beyond where you are now?" he asked me.

I tend to be reticent when in the company of my father's people. I didn't think much of Brother Raleigh's question then. But at home words and actions are great signifiers that connote so much deeper meaning than we think on the surface. The last I heard of Raleigh was that he was still in Ekiadolor and though he owned so many hectares of land before the area became developed, he had not changed his economic status much. I understand he complained of money to attend the extended Ojaide family's bi-monthly meeting, hence he was not showing up. He must believe in something keeping him down. He must believe from his remarks that I could have advanced further in my career, if there was general consent of the Ojaide family. His mistrust of the family's goodwill to him and others made me believe that the firstborn was always under attack. He is his father's firstborn male. As for me, though my father's firstborn male, I think all I need is the Almighty's grace. After all, our people who believe so much in witchcraft say that it is in the same town that there are so many witches that centenarians thrive! There are always exceptions and I believe strongly in eluding the family traps for the firstborn male!

In my maternal side, I heeded the call for a family meeting for reconciliation. I was to be reconciled with a cousin I had never taken to despite our being raised in the same compound. He was my senior uncle's firstborn male. He had cast aspersions on our grandfather and complained of his dislike of the name he had given to his first son as I had given my grandmother's name to my second daughter. Later that son might have been involved in some underworld activity in which he never returned. In any case, my cousin was asked to apologize for a malicious remark that he had made that my junior womb sister had overheard.

"If we had known then that he would be like this, it would have been possible to eliminate him!"

"That type of statement comes from the mouth of a witch," my uncle's senior wife said.

"He must apologize," many others insisted.

My cousin and uncle kept quiet. As for my uncle, I could not tell whether he was playing the diplomatic game or not. After all, he stood for me, as my mother's immediate brother, as father on the maternal side. My cousin was his nephew as I was.

One event begot another. During my uncle's burial, my junior sister would chastise me for coming from that far away with my wife and for spending so much money for who kept mum when somebody was savaging me with wicked feelings before him.

"He couldn't even condemn him before all of us," my sister said.

I have learnt to listen much and talk less or keep mum at home. It suffices for me to do the right thing.

The last time I had been to my father's home was some twenty-four years earlier. That was before the burial of my father-in-law and I came personally to invite my people to accompany me to the burial ceremony at Ekakpamre. When my mother-in-law died, I sent my brother Ese to tell them. They had grumbled that I should have come personally to inform them but I told them I was too busy to come. I sent a bus and a lorry to pick those who wanted to come, and they came in droves. They helped me to fill the place, enliven the occasion, and make my appearance at my late mother-in-law's burial very successful. One's relations always have a place in one's life and they did me a good turn that I will not forget. As the elders say, "Avwe ohwo vwovwo kere amwa." I had used my relatives and friends to cover myself as a good wrapper!

I knew my father's spirit yearned to see me in the family home. I knew my father would be happy I was not lost in any wilderness but came home. I was not going to go on footpaths as I did when Ubrukpokpo, my senior cousin, literally led me by the hand to my father's home just before I was five. I was going home as an adult and in a different mode. While at Ibadan as an undergraduate, it always surprised me that the day after I arrived at home—Ibada Village—my father always came to visit. I never sent word ahead home that I was coming but somehow he knew. Whenever I asked him how he knew, he smiled in his measured way.

"Are you not my son?" he asked.

"Yes, I am."

"I feel it when you are coming. And then I see you in my dream here at home!" he had told me.

Even as I prepared to come from the United States, I knew my father though dead knew I was coming home and would be expecting me at Enemarho Village. As I left Effurun, I knew that great seer though dead already knew his son was on his way to the village. Later thought of him knowing I was coming home gave me a sense of security that I would be safe at home.

The journey started from picking my mother and brother, Erhire, to join me in the visit. There was a new road to start with—no longer passing through Okurekpo and veering left from the old market. Rather, we faced Eku and branched at the intersection of the new tarred road that joined or was supposed to join Okpara Inland and Okpara Waterside. Like every government project in this area, it was jinxed. After driving barely two kilometers on the Okpara Inland Road, we turned left. The small villages of the olden days that were thriving appeared now to be evacuated of human beings and filled with grass. What should be an inter-town road has become a bush path with tall grasses that slapped the car as I drove through the pot-holed road. How could a place be worse off today than it was some fifty years ago? For sure the thriving villages of Okurehavwo, Okurunoh, and others where we held social gatherings in those days have lost their young ones to Warri, Sapele, and other urban centers. Even I could not see old people as I drove along. Maybe people did not live till old age in the area anymore because of the seeming hardship. Many times I had learnt as a young man that the contract for the road from Okurekpo through these villages to Samagidi had been awarded by the State Government but the contractors always, always "chopped" the money and did nothing. It was the jinx of local roads contracted by Government for tarring; they suffered the same fate of abandonment.

I no longer knew the road. Fortunately, Emmanuel sat in front, while my mother, Jonathan, and Erhire sat behind. Emmanuel, my maternal uncle's son, had joined me at my mother's house to be part of the trip. We passed Okurehavwo, where Esther once a village beauty lived; she is now married and lives in Okpara Inland, I understand. I have not heard anything about her sister, Felicia. The place was bush and no longer a village. The same fate befell Okurunoh where we used to hold social gatherings. It reminded me of Gregory, a sharp mind that appears lost in the wilderness of America. We passed the tiny Oko Isoko that had houses slumping or already down and overgrown with weeds. Ivworho Village was shrunk to several compounds surrounded by tall weeds. I asked for the big cherry tree in what used to be Orhonise's Compound. That cherry tree cheered up young ones and its fruits had Orhonise's trademark of sweetness. It had been mowed down by overzealous pastors who said it was coven where witches plotted the demise of progressive people in the area, I was told. After Oko Aka, we entered my father's village which I could not recognize but I knew was before Inayegue's Village, where mad folks were cured through physical beating and herbal drugs by the medicine-man Inayegue, after whom the village was named. He must have achieved results because mad men and women were brought from far and near for him to cure.

Emmanuel pointed at my father's house or rather the house I rebuilt for my father. I stopped in front of the house as if I knew it very well. From then on I had to behave as if I was familiar with the place. It was a two bedroom bungalow with a large sitting room. Ohwode, a distant cousin, lives in and maintains the house and the compound. It was neatly furnished and well maintained. The compound was clean also. He had taken good care of the house. I surveyed the house and saw plastic chairs neatly packed in one corner. I knew that the plastic chairs I had bought to please the gods of the extended Ojaide family were there for their sons and daughters to sit on at meetings and rent out for burial and wedding ceremonies to make some money for the family.

As custom demanded, I had to go round to greet every household in the depleted village. It was surely depleted of human beings, depleted of animals, depleted of liveliness, and depleted of much more I cannot now describe. I could barely recognize the village. What twenty-four or so years have done to ravage a thriving village! My father's village was fast becoming a ghost village but for the wrinkled women around. I did not see old men around. They must have all joined the ancestors early enough rather than continue living in the hole. My father had called it a hole even when it was thriving and did not want me to live there. Imagine now that it has become a real hole in the forest! Alfred was now the senior male in the village. Perhaps two or three years older than me, he looked older than his real years. He had been hardened and wrinkled by the harsh rural environment, I suppose. The only other folks were women.

Children stared at me. Wives, almost all married the past twenty-four years or so, stared at me.

"Is he Emoghware?" they asked their seniors.

I must have been talked about for so long without being seen. Yes, I am their Emoghware, son of Dafetanure. I am their Professor. I didn't know how I had been imagined by the children and women who heard about me but had never seen me before now. I must have been a hero to the children who might have heard I had gone abroad to study and got a Ph.D., the first boy from the village to get a doctoral degree, become a Professor, and win literary prizes. I am just one of them and many of those children, boys and girls, could go farther than me, if their parents direct them and they are determined. And they are lucky! One has to be lucky in many ways. Many bright young men and women from the village or villages around attended the same St. Charles Primary School, Okurekpo, with me but had not gone far because of their parents' lack of direction. Of course, many fathers chose to marry more wives rather than put their children in secondary school, as my father did.

Sitting down in my father's house furnished by Ohwode, my mother asked me to send for a bottle of Schnapps which I had brought together with other bottles of gin, a carton of Star beer and a crate of soft drinks. I then poured libation over my father's grave.

"Take this from me for constantly taking care of me. Thank you for taking me to places and back safely. You have been a great protector and guide when alive and dead," I murmured.

I knew he has continued to protect me from beyond. My mind shot back to my first visit to Enemarho Village when my maternal cousin, Ubrukpokpo, held me by the hand to hand me over from my Grandma to my father. The first night in my father's house, he cut me with a razor blade and rubbed some unguents on the bloody spots. It was painful but I did not ask for what reason he did that—somehow I knew it was for my good because Grandma had done that to cure me of frequent convulsions, she had later explained to me. Dafetanure knew from the beginning how to protect his son in the battlefield of the society. When he visited me in Ibada Village, he used to warn me against the hunchback, the witch, he feared the most because she intimidated all by calling herself "Aeroplane."

"Go to your coven and fly in your groundnut shell, you witch!" my father would mutter in rejection of her bewitching spell.

Aeroplane and those my father feared had all died. They must all be in Ancestors' Land where they should have rid themselves of rancor and bitterness after a lifetime of conflict and petty jealousies. They all should be silent in peace now. The village has rid itself of poison, witchcraft, and other bad things that their lives meant to each other. I was in another Enemarho Village; though depleted but not fearsome.

The house soon filled up as word went round that I was visiting. Cellphones were ringing, no doubt transmitting the news of the return of the prodigal son. Talking drums had been withdrawn from service since the appearance of Nokia mobile phones. Yes, you could reach so many people within a short time. Times have changed that the remotest of villages, what my father would have liked to describe as holes, had access to phones. Ohwode had already called my nephew, Duke, who lived in Onumane, a Kokori village. I was formally welcomed back home with kola nuts, drinks, and money. Everybody come to welcome us added some money. I was impressed and cheered by the goodwill of my people, men, women, and children. After their welcome, it was my turn to place on the table what I had brought: kola nuts, drinks, and some money to be shared among my hosts and hostesses, the men, women, and youths present. It was a reunion that thrilled me as it thrilled my hosts.

As it got to late afternoon, my mother signaled that it was getting late and we should ask for permission to depart. I called Ohwode to brief me on any issues he wanted me to know about. He pointed at the burrow pit and railroad that passed my father's land. I had heard of that burrow pit where Ibobo's son had drowned. He also showed me the new Baptist Church, the only church in the village. It was established by Professor Uvie Igun, my friend, who had been Vice Chancellor at Delta State University but now on contract teaching at Niger Delta University, Amassoma. I was surprised at the choice of Enemarho as the place to build the Baptist Church. Uvie has become a Baptist evangelist and goes to the church most Sundays. Even before I came for this visit, he had been talking about my father's house which I had not seen. He was able to convert Ohwode who now attends the new church.

Ohwode also briefed me on my father's lands and many rubber plantations. Dafetanure had tried his hands at many things. He was the only Urhobo man I knew as a young man who cultivated cocoa and coffee. I still have strong memories of the cocoa and coffee farm close to the old house he moved from to the new Enemarho Village. The aroma of the lush farm still stays with me. My father was also a palm oil producer and I still have a mental picture of his palm oil press deep in the bush and farther from the village than his rubber plantation. Dafetanure was a meticulous man who brought whatever he did to native perfection. He produced the best palm oil. As for his rubber, he made A1 rubber sheets with a science native to his head. He took his time in whatever he did to bring it to perfection.

I asked Ohwode to use whatever money he got from there to take care of the house and the compound but must report to my mother. He could plant whatever he liked for himself and others who wanted to farm in my father's land should get permission from him or my mother. If he needed to improve on the house, he should let me know. He must not allow my father's house to go into disrepair; he must not hesitate to ask me for money when necessary to take care of the place.

As we stood outside ready to depart, I had to see more people individually. Some I gave money, others I took their cellphone numbers. We hopped into the car and drove off. It was a great day for me and, and I believe, for my fellow Enemarho Villagers who had come to welcome me. I had overcome the fear of going home and entered my father's house. The firstborn male has come home to reclaim his heritage.

3

INSIDE THE NIGERIAN ACADEMY

I left the United States with excitement that I was going to contribute to the Nigerian university system. After all, each in his or her own way and where most appropriate. I am a product of Nigerian universities, having attended the University of Ibadan in the late sixties to the very early seventies at a crucial time in Nigerian history—the Civil War period. That was when most Nigerian universities could hold their own beside any good university in the world. That was when Ibadan was not only Nigeria's but Africa's premier university. I believe I went through the university as much as the university went through me. By the time I would go to Syracuse University in Upstate New York in the United States, I felt I had received better training than my American counterparts in my Creative Writing and English classes. My professors made me feel so and I felt very confident in a foreign institution.

Since the mid-1980s, things started to change. Frequent military dictators did not care about the quality of education and might have reduced the budgets for running the universities. They did not make salaries competitive with other jobs within the country and especially salaries of Nigerian university teachers were peanuts, so to say, compared with salaries paid to their colleagues in other African universities, not to talk of colleagues in the UK or North America. That was when the exodus began—a flight of some of the brightest minds in the Nigerian academy then. Nigerian academics took up teaching jobs in Ghana, The Gambia, Libya, Swaziland, Botswana, and South Africa, among other African nations. I understand some academics went to Europe to take up menial jobs that were paying more than lecturers' salaries in Nigeria. However, the flight to the United States was even more.

Many of the bright minds are now professors in American universities. There is barely any university or college in the United States without several Nigerian academics. In fact, many left Nigeria during the military regimes of Idiagbon-Buhari, Ibrahim Babangida, and Sani Abacha. At that time, instead of measures that would keep these academics at home, the Government was attributed to saying that "let those who want to go away go away!" It is sad because when the United States Government and institutions were issuing accelerated "Green Cards" and citizenship to Nigerian academics, the Nigerian Government should have known that there was something appealing to Americans in these Nigerians that it was losing. By the time the Obasanjo civilian administration attempted to make salaries living wages, the damage had already been done to the universities with university teachers looking for other ways beside their salaries to survive. Of course, that affected their morale and the quality of their teaching and the "products" they brought out of their institutions.

The reality in Nigeria thus degraded the high quality of institutions there before the mid-1980s. Frequent student and faculty strikes have disrupted learning, teaching, and research. Increase in salaries of teachers and administrative staff has not shown an equal rise in the quality of graduates coming out of the institutions. In rankings of African universities very few Nigerian universities appear among the first fifty and of course in the world rankings of the universities, no Nigerian university is listed among the best two hundred. By 2013 I knew I was going back to Nigeria when the reputation of Nigerian universities had plummeted to an all-time low with degrees of many universities being questioned within and outside the country.

I had taught in many Nigerian universities, especially at the University of Maiduguri from 1977 to 1989. The University had sent me to Syracuse for my MA in Creative

Writing and Ph.D. in English. Then, Unimaid, as the university was popularly known, was a respected university whose Vice Chancellor would later be tapped to be not only Minister of Education but also Minister of Petroleum Resources of the Federal Republic of Nigeria. I have gone back to teach at the University of Maiduguri, which was no longer what it used to be but declining fast. It had the look of a declining but minimally functioning university in 2002/2003. In that academic year I had split my teaching between two universities, spending a semester at Maiduguri and the other semester at Delta State University, Abraka. I also have other university teaching experiences in Nigeria. For some two years, when Professor Chris Ikporikpo was Vice Chancellor at Niger Delta University, Amassoma, Bayelsa State, I had a special arrangement to teach there during the summer from about May 1 to late August. At another time, the Fall Semester of 2008, I also taught at Delta State University at Abraka. These teaching experiences were in addition to my making presentations or reading from my work at the University of Lagos, the University of Nigeria, the University of Abuja, Ado Bayero University, and the University of Uyo, among so many. I thus have familiar knowledge of Nigerian universities.

During the year of my new fellowship, I was supposed to teach at the University of Abuja. I was supposed to teach creative writing, supposed to teach African poetry, supposed to teach American literature. Yes, there was much I was supposed to do. However, once I arrived in Nigeria, everything I had planned to do in Abuja became things I was supposed to do. I had planned to teach undergraduate and graduate students upon arrival and I had taken along books on theory and other aspects of literature I felt would be difficult to lay hands on when in Nigeria. What I had planned to do at the University of Abuja was done in my University of North Carolina at Charlotte's office of a twenty-first century organized research university. I planned inside a university that had not witnessed a strike in all my twenty-five years there. I planned to teach in Nigeria in an American university where there is always a five-year calendar that has never been disrupted in all my twenty-five years in the system. I planned in a stable institution what to do in an unstable system. That was how things turned out to be. What I planned to do had become what I was supposed to do.

My correspondence had been with the Head of Department of English and, of course, she received me warmly. As soon as I arrived at Abuja, I told her about setting up an appointment to see the Vice Chancellor.

"I'll like to book an appointment to see the VC on my own or with you," I told my Head of Department.

"You don't need to book an appointment to see him. We can go and wait to see him; if he is there, we'll see him. You never can tell when he'll be in the office. I don't think his office staff members know either," she said.

I was surprised that we did not need to book an appointment to see him but just have to wait to see the CEO of the University of Abuja.

We went the following day, a Tuesday, to the VC's office. There I learnt that sometimes he worked from home and he invited academic staff to see him at home. We arrived at about 10 a.m. and were seated in the waiting room with torn and moldy chairs. The room, where visitors were supposed to have a foretaste of the main office, had dust-laden fans and I could tell that there was no electric light on at the time. The stained walls had marks of a leaking roof. Despite the outer office teeming with workers, the floor did not seem to have been swept. I believe roaches would party there at night and make occasional raids to seize food left behind in the office.

Fortunately, we learnt that the VC was coming to the office that day. "Hurray!" I shouted in my mind, for being lucky not to have wasted my trip to the campus from town. It appears there was no specific time for him to be in the office.

He came when he came! He passed through the waiting room into his office. Everybody stood up to salute the chief. He shook hands with as many as he could and everybody trooped after him into his large office. The office desk is perhaps the largest I have ever seen in an office. Files were placed in some disorderly manner that perhaps made sense to him or his secretary.

"Yes, you!" he beckoned on my HOD.

"Sir, here is our Fulbright fellow," she was saying and was interrupted by the chief.

"What is he here for?"

"To teach in our Department," she lamely answered.

Before she finished, the VC was talking to another person, apparently a contractor from the question about when a specific work would be completed.

"He needs accommodation," my HOD shouted over the contractor.

"Yes, we'll provide him accommodation. There are many houses in Abuja where he can live," he said, as if every house in Abuja was open to me to live in.

Since I was given no accommodation despite the many promises of the VC who had genuflected to the Executive Secretary of the Nigerian University Commission promising him that he would provide me accommodation, I stayed in a hotel at my own expense for the first two weeks. I visited the VC's office again. He came in and I was told to wait till he would call me. By the time I had stayed over forty minutes, I had become suspicious that I had waited too long for an executive officer who, from my earlier visit, seemed to relish receiving visitors who would praise him for his vice-chancellorship, even if many others would see him as doing nothing to improve the university and even running down the institution.

"I have been waiting for so long to see the VC," I told the Secretary.

"Sorry Sir, he has gone to the airport," she told me.

"Nonsense, how could he keep me waiting here and steal away?" I asked.

Perhaps the Secretary had not heard anybody use the word "Nonsense" to describe the action of the VC before her and so looked at me perhaps wondering what man in the university dared be rude to her boss. The university chief had stolen out of his office through another door without my knowing. I had had enough by the fourth week in Abuja. I could not rent any apartment, since landlords wanted me to pay for one full year or two years in advance. I could not live in Abuja on a regular basis staying in hotels which were very expensive. I had to split ten months between Abuja and Effurun, between teaching and research.

It is easy to say what I will observe is generalized but that is because I don't want to be too specific for obvious reasons. It is possible that members of the Nigerian academy or others will ask me to mention where I experienced some specific happenings I hope to narrate. Still, others might ask me to tell in what universities the lecturers and professors I talk about are teaching. What is important to me, from my firsthand experience recently, is the reflection of the Nigerian academy which for the most part needs serious restructuring and revamping in academic and non-academic staff and infrastructures. Of course, there should be exceptions to the campuses and the professors that I describe. It might be I met the wrong set of academics, but I acknowledge there could be many good and committed university teachers I did not meet.

We had been warned at the orientation conducted through Webinar for those going to Nigeria in particular to expect university strikes and prepare to do research or some other things when such happened. I knew that Nigerian state universities are prone to long strikes. I flew into one of such strikes. Strikes are so common in Nigeria that one can say they are endemic. There are strikes by medical doctors at times of serious epidemics—their Hippocratic oaths matter not when they need more money. There are strikes of judicial workers at a time of election petitions. There is a strike of university teachers almost all the time. Often the strikes are for more pay in the forms of salary raises or unpaid allowances. On the other side of strikes are governments, federal and state, that have a penchant for reneging on signed agreements. To the strikers, government behaves like a trickster or even a fraudster. Once strikers go back to work, the government feels it has succeeded in pushing forward implementing agreements that relate to more budgetary allocations for salary increase or infrastructure development. The students are caught up in the governments-university teachers' union's frequent battles.

Coming from a different university culture, I find it difficult to understand why salaries for different positions are not fixed at specific amounts. Rather, there are so many ways to arrive at a teacher's salary. Why should university teachers still be paid houseboys' and gardeners' allowances, as if still in colonial times when Britain ruled Nigeria? Unless, the university teachers are expatriates in their home country! There are allowances for supervising graduate (also called postgraduate) students. What is a university teacher there for, if not to teach and supervise students? I am surprised those allowances sought have not included car allowances or some other types of stipend to pay for the dresses the teachers wear to the classroom! This is not to ridicule the teachers but the pay structure needs to be renegotiated and brought to contemporary university standards in a global world and taking into cognizance the national economy and other groups of workers. In other words, without the shenanigans of allowances for house boys, gardeners, transportation, and housing, why can't the salary be fixed or negotiated at a certain amount and with levels within each rank? It is ludicrous to see the breakdown of university teachers' salaries as they are currently calculated in Nigeria.

I can understand why university teachers have frequent strikes and sometimes appear unyielding before a stubborn, insensitive and corrupt government. Yes, they strike for pay because in Nigeria it is money that not only pays one's bills but also grants one prestige. If the local government chairman or any of the supervisors earns so much and shares so much of the quarterly allocations from the Federal Government without accountability, why should university teachers, especially professors, not earn something commensurate with their education? If state assemblymen and women earn so much and share so much in committees, as the public believes, why should university teachers not earn more than the state or federal government pays them? There is no need to compare university teachers with federal assemblymen and women and senators who raise their own salaries in secret meetings. Rumors, the only thing you can rely on in this case of secrecy, say they could earn as much as between eleven and fifteen million naira a month. The same legislators would resist raising the minimum wage for a worker from eighteen thousand naira a month! But there is the admission that Nigerian politicians are the highest paid on earth—more than those of the United States, Germany, Japan, or other developed economies. They are fat cats of a special breed. And that's upon the self-awarded contracts for jobs that could only be done and paid for on paper!

One more thought about the ASUU strikes. I would expect the strikers to think more of aspects of the academy that would enhance their knowledge, productivity, and quality of teaching. Those areas seem to be often forgotten in these strikes or appear drowned in the calls for salary raises. The ASUU Public Relations machine is weak and it cannot articulate many grievances which the public always thinks are about pay hikes. I lost a great friend and writer in the last strike—Festus Iyayi. He was driving to Kano for an executive committee meeting when near Lokoja the convoy of a governor caused his car to somersault and he died on the spot of the accident. Rumors and social media have it that he was shot since there were bullet holes to his chest. There was no probe and no criminal action taken against the members of the Kogi State Governor's convoy that caused his death. That was in Nigerian style where the police and military still have immunity against prosecution in a civilian regime. Festus, a great democrat and worker, was a casualty of the ASUU strike. A little later the tortoise government signed another agreement with the ASUU to implement what it had agreed to in 2009! I will not be surprised if the tortoise lives to its kind and ASUU will be compelled to call another strike for the implementation of another signed agreement.

As you enter the campus of this university, unkempt guards open the gate. Seven to eight guards, five to six too many, dressed in dark blue uniform open the metal gate. One or two of the guards hand over plastic cards to take into the campus and drop at the gate before being allowed to leave the other side of the gate. There, some check the trunk of cars and others raise or lower the iron bar crossing the out-road. On entering, there's the farce of one of the guards seemingly writing down car plate numbers coming into the campus. That is, the hub of the campuses numbered 1, 2, and 3, according to the time they were built. Campus 1 started in colonial times and bears the mark of a teachers' college whose kind no longer exists. However, the buildings, as you will expect of colonial times, stood stronger than those of Campus 2, the postcolonial construct of greed—ramshackle buildings that contractors and administrators built with huge sums of money but below every standard of a university building. The third campus will be another story since I saw the initial plans when the then Commissioner for Education visited the then Vice Chancellor with a contractor ready to build the new campus without the university's contribution to the plan. But let me come back to Campus 2, my entrance to the university.

That is an impossible task for someone with a camera to do, not to talk of one using long hand to write down the plate numbers of the stream of cars entering the campus in the early morning rush hour. Of course, the clumsy man in a guard's uniform is not a robot either to accomplish the mechanical task. I noticed that as he used long hand, perhaps barely literate, to write down one car's plate number, more than three to four cars have passed without his looking up. Security, university style!

Dust was everywhere and as fine cars of professors passed, a dust bowl was raised. So many jeeps filled the haphazard parking areas which were not demarcated. Over ninety-nine percent of these cars and jeeps were second-hand but were taken good care of and appeared new. Drivers parked their cars under trees, across footpaths, and anywhere there was space. There was no sense of order or managing space. Big jeeps, gas guzzlers, stopped and the drivers jumped down to open the back doors for the professors or university officials to come out. The driver would then carry bags of their *oga* bosses to their offices. As the big man alighted, there were choruses of "Prof, Prof" everywhere. Even friends called their colleagues "Prof" and not their birth names.

It is an egotistical culture. I have heard of professors who do not respond to greetings from their junior colleagues or students and seem to be like walking zombies to mystify their professorship. Some nod to respond to "Good morning, Prof!" Others wave their hands like politicians at rallies or even like the Pope waving at a universal congregation from his Pope-Mobile. A few professors go as far as responding to greetings verbally, choosing to save themselves from moving their hands or heads by saying "Hello, my dear!" Where they got this greeting, I know not but it seems the rank of professorship has turned into a cult whose members invent bizarre ways of demeaning the underlings who greet them. I know of new professors who ask whether they are walking or behaving like *profs* should! But in a country where at big parties some people like to be introduced as Professor High Chief Anything, Engineer Nobody, Architect Stupidity, Accountant Broke, Surveyor Missroad, and so forth, I was not surprised to see the pomposity of professors, some of whom may not have the substance of an entering good Assistant Professor.

That is, from the way they get their professorship. There are daughters and sons of the soil—indigenes of the area who want to be promoted because they are from where the university is located. Such tend to use their ethnicity to advantage by threatening to cause or really sow seeds of ethnic discord that fouls the campus atmosphere. There are wives and mistresses of the top hierarchy who are latched with a few sound ones into the pinnacle of academia. There are also those in the VC's camp, cheerleaders who get their reward for supporting the VC at all cost and however incompetently and corruptly he or she administers the institution. "Amraibure" is a common name in the area. I have seen so many of their kind that I can give an unending list of their sort.

I witnessed a laughable scene in a Senate meeting in which one of the VC's praise-singers, after singing his boss's praises as the best VC ever not only of that university but of all Nigerian universities, tabled a motion that the VC should remain in office forever! He knew that the office was for five years and the specific VC had barely a year left in his tenure but so brainless though a professor he wanted to tickle the fancy of the VC who smiled broadly and even joined most of the Senate members who stood to give the griot of a professor a standing ovation. A poor griot for that matter because the true one feeds his audience with the milk of truth! I remained in my seat and laughed. The type of Obasanjo's laughter over his former Vice President's fantasy of becoming the nation's President! There are exceptions because I observe that the very sound academics tend to be self-effacing, modest, and not noisy.

I have heard of professors or Senior Lecturers or Associate Professors who supervise students and take money from them. Some ask for their graduate students to buy tires for their cars. I have heard one student say they contributed money for the professor's summer vacation in the United States. Others virtually contributed the funds for the burial of a professor's father! Many receive expensive gifts and some use their female students as mistresses. Many graduate students contribute money to pay External Examiners since the authorities might not pay the examiners on time, if at all. Some lecturers take money from their students. Of course, by so doing, they ignore professionalism and graduate many mediocre students in their disciplines.

Like everywhere there are weak professors, there are also strong ones. It is from the same environment that the weak ones complain about the lack of research materials or inability to work that some distinguish themselves. Almost in all the universities I know in Nigeria there are serious scholars who can stand up to their counterparts elsewhere in the world. Such ones partake in the rewards of academic industry. I met several lecturers who have published sound books on their research. Others win external fellowships and grants, which a majority of the university faculty members do not even know exist. To those who are able to surmount local difficulties and join the global world of academia, I salute their diligence.

The classrooms and offices in many of the universities are not conducive for learning but some VCs continue as emperors the Nero style—fiddling while Rome burnt. I have witnessed lectures under trees, in the open, or in hovels called classrooms. I once taught at a mini-stadium because there were no classrooms. In the universities I know, class teaching does not take precedence over other meetings as I know in the United States. Weekend programs, sandwich programs, and other money-making programs take precedence over what should be the regular university programs. Academics are told to attend faculty meetings and not go to class. There is a litany of wrong things taking place that need to be fixed in the academy. Things can be better conducted in these institutions.

I need to make a few more remarks on the Nigerian academy. I had planned to do a workshop to teach university teachers how to write peer-reviewed essays and proposals for grants and fellowships. I should have visited the National University Commission over five times but nothing seemed to be happening. I even wrote a state Commissioner of Education who used to be a university teacher and whom I know for funds to organize it. The Commissioner said there was no money. I was invited to a party in the State capital where money would be wasted for nothing and I declined it. By early February, I heard from the NUC. The Commission was having ideas as mine to organize a workshop and they had arranged one and I should be one of the resource persons to talk on writing peer-reviewed essays and grant proposals. Was I going to be angry that someone had hijacked my ideas? I was interested in making sure that as many as possible in the academy knew these things. I went to the workshop and made my presentation. The attendance was rather poor and the irony of it was that it was mainly the private universities that sent their teachers to the workshop. I was privileged to be in a screening group for Fulbright fellows from Nigeria going to the United States for study. Many from the private universities did even better than those from state and federal universities. I don't know whether or not it was a matter of those who knew about the program and so applied and so each university should have a medium of communicating fellowship opportunities to its staff. It is through learning that we know things! Without learning, we are lost or mired in ignorance.

And things are worse when we resist learning what we don't know and claim to know.

Most of the full professors seem to work the least in the university. Many choose to do the least teaching. And that is not because they are doing research but out of sheer laziness. One professor has made it known that he does not get out of bed until 9 a.m. because he has to watch his *Africa Magic* program till late in the night. He says he does not have the time to read any big book. Others sit before the television watching English Premier League and European Club matches till very late and have more knowledge of those teams, their managers, players, and history than what they are professors of. Many farm out their courses to those they supervise or junior faculty to teach for them. A female professor who is not known outside that university and boasts as an expert in an aspect of language passes her courses to graduate students she herself describes as mediocre. Some professors, out of greed, take courses to teach from the Open University or weekend and sandwich programs but do not enter the classroom a single day! They coerce the graduate students they supervise or junior lecturers who will rely on their recommendations for promotion to teach them while they receive the salaries. There are others who do not even grade the exams they set but give the student scripts to junior academics or graduate students to grade for them.

I also observe that there is very little or none of mentoring of junior academics by the Profs, despite all the harangues as professors. Junior academics do not know what to do to advance in the profession and just wander about aimlessly in the academic wilderness. Many young academics do not know how to write peer-reviewed articles. Nor do they know how to write proposals for grants or fellowships. The point is that if gold rusts, what will iron do? The professors themselves do not know or are generally outdated in their writings. There appears, from my personal observation, in where I taught and elsewhere that the university teachers are too concerned with looking for ways to make money that their university jobs suffer irreparably from their greed.

If the National University Commission should audit the full professors in Nigeria, it will discover that perhaps half of them have not published in a peer-reviewed article the past five or more years. That is not to talk of writing a book! That was an argument that should have been raised when ASUU negotiated with the Government for the retirement age of professors to be raised from sixty-five to seventy. If folks are already deadwood in their fifties, why should they go beyond sixty-five unless tested from their research or publication and teaching? And university teachers, irrespective of their ranks, who are productive, teach well, and healthy should be given the chance to continue their career even if older than seventy if they choose to do so.

I was in the company of a female professor when some other academics asked her what she was still doing in the university. There ought to be a system to review the performance of university teachers whatever their rank. Those that are unproductive have to be warned and if they continued to be so should be retired whatever their age.

"You are already a professor-o! Make you go look for appointment and leave this work for us," they advised.

She told me that was common advice to her since she got promoted to full professorship. And that is what many of them are doing—spending their time lobbying for political appointments where they could preside over stupendous budgets without being accountable to anybody. They could go to the NUC or TET Fund or Raw Materials, NACA, and so many parastatals that the Federal or state governments pour so much money into without a clear idea of what to get from them. Many become commissioners at State levels, run for offices and often lose or lobby hard to be political advisers to half-literate corrupt politicians.

Students in Nigerian universities suffer from so many inadequacies. Even weak students could become learned if they had good teachers. It appears to me that the students are eager to learn. I taught courses in American literature and creative writing and I was amazed at the students' passion for learning. Of course, I am from the USA and maybe they know I am from elsewhere and their keen enthusiasm gladdened my heart. I made them feel they could learn by studying. They wrote essays, made oral presentations in class. They typed their essays, since I insisted I wanted professionally written essays. While in the American literature class, a group of students, mainly girls, always answered questions; I found the students very amiable. Just before the end of the semester, the students organized a group photograph which I still keep and cherish till today. My point is that given the right atmosphere and resources, these Nigerian students are as good as my American students. That is, if the many professors would descend from their divine pinnacle to teach the students as they are supposed to and are paid for in a university setting with state-of-the-art infrastructures!

I had the same experience of my creative writing class however short the period at the University of Abuja. Students wrote freely expressing themselves mainly in poetry and short stories. Even when I asked for a poem or two and typed, many students went to write and submit three and even four. We established a wonderful rapport and I told them that whether as scholars or writers, they should always feel free to contact me.

One way of empowering the students before their teachers should be for a mandatory student evaluation of every course they are taught. I understand some universities are already doing it, but it is random and the result is not used for anything. If student evaluations are used for the promotion of their teachers, the Profs would not be missing so many classes. I have heard of professors or senior academics not going to class till several weeks to the exam when they go to the class to tell the students what to prepare for the exams in courses they have not taught. If the university authorities also put in place a merit pay raise system in place for teachers that teach well and publish in peer-reviewed articles, and win grants, the university standard of education would surely be raised.

I have some other observations on the campuses. In many campuses there is the proliferation of prayer groups. In one institution, as I took my morning walk at about 5:45 a.m., I heard bedlam in the female students' hostels. I understand they wake to pray together from 5:30 to 6 a.m. I thought if at all they wanted to pray, those interested should have gone to their church and there are many empty buildings to go to at that hour to shout their wishes to God. They have coerced every resident of the hostels into their faith and prevented others from sleeping or reading. In that university, I have been told of students, who on the eve of their examinations, go to spend the night in their churches to pray to pass. Or they go there early to be blessed by the pastors and rush from the church to the examination hall believing they are still filled with the Holy Spirit that would make them perform well in the exam. Of course, they have abandoned their reading and preparing for the exam. In another tertiary institution, many students resort to the "morning call" and address the empty air shouting. Some of the students "speak in tongues" but are really blabbering nonsense. A stranger would take them to be madmen and women roaming the grounds of higher institutions. Every event, including Senate, Faculty, and Departmental Meetings must begin and end with prayers invoking Jesus to steer the group to do things aright even as most of the campus is festering in corruption of all kinds. Many universities or faculties/colleges devote one day in the week for prayer sessions, where the pastor/priest lecturers preside for hours praying as if the Almighty is deaf and is not aware of the shenanigans of the campus.

One would ask, what are Nigerian universities doing in research and contributing to knowledge? In the humanities and social sciences, what research is being done to transform the society? Looking at doctoral works, one shakes one's head. The supervisors and departments look over their local problems to foreign issues to research on. Often they ignore, neglect, or don't even see what needs to be studied in the immediate community. Many universities should ask themselves, what transformation have they brought to their home towns? There is so much to research on in the Nigerian landscape but often looked over. The scientists should make serious effort to solve the many problems. How would Africans be waiting for universities in Edinburgh or Atlanta to produce the cure for malaria that our people have always suffered from? Are the universities making the effort to reduce diseases and poverty in their midst? If they are universities, why are they not doing what universities do elsewhere? I have on an occasion questioned a doctoral student who was defending a thesis why a Ph.D. in English was being done according to a format that was not the MLA's. He told me that that was the way it was done in the university irrespective of the discipline. I asked him why a doctoral degree in English, Sociology, and Pharmacy should not follow the formats of their respective disciplines and I was told "if you do the right thing here, you will fail!" And so they follow blindly. There is a certain abominable rigidity and a lack of flexibility to contemporary change and being current with issues. The result of this is that many of the universities in Nigeria seem to be many years behind the rest of the world.

There has to be changes in the Nigerian academy for things to improve. The university teachers should affirm faith in their institutions. There are university teachers and commissioners of education who send their children overseas. If they think they are doing a great job, why not have their children or wards where they teach? Ukraine, Cyprus, Ghana,

South Africa, Malaysia, Britain, Canada, and the United States seem to be the destinations for study of the children of many university staff and government officials.

I also feel much effort should be put on improving infrastructures on campuses, from libraries to laboratories and state-of-the-art classrooms. There should be discipline so that students should not waste time when new semesters begin. From my observation, it seems much time is lost as students tend to take their time when universities reopen. Often time is wasted on registration which could be done faster than presently done.

The problems of Nigerian universities are mainly systemic. After all, the universities are part of the country bedeviled by systemic problems. The universities need constant electricity and most of them cannot afford to run their own electricity outside the national grid. Many universities and other tertiary institutions do not have constant water also and one sees students carrying plastic buckets looking for where to fetch water for their use. Also, as Nigeria's problem stems from leadership, so are university problems. The development of each university is allied to the performance of the vice chancellor. The more selfless the vice chancellor, the more done and the more greedy he or she is, the less done in the university. Governing Councils should endeavor to select professors who are role models to head their institutions to see positive results.

4

RICH PASTORS, POOR AND SICK CONGREGATIONS

Leaving Abuja for Effurun, Delta State, I was bound to come close to pastors, priests, venerable ones, prophets, evangelists, miracle workers, and a host of men of god. I arrived as one bishop, who was the executive head of his own church, was making waves on mouth-to-mouth news in the Effurun-Warri area. He had been going on crusades, the story went, and he usually burnt down traditional shrines in every village or town he visited. His overzealous assistants accompanied him with jerry cans of fuel to be ready for the destruction of Satan's habitats. To his followers, Satan lived in shrines in groves that were found in almost every town. Once the villagers had been intimidated about Satan causing them to be steeped in poverty and disease, the bishop would raise songs and, under possession, flames would consume the shrine. Many felt he might be absorbing the powers of the gods of those shrines that he destroyed. That power could be mystical, diabolic, or even, ironically, Satanic!

He hit a brick wall at Kokori, where he wanted to destroy the people's warrior god's shrine. Egba, in recent times, had been linked to kidnapers the god protected but that did not make his devotees to abandon him. There was a rallying call from the non-believers to defend their god. Egba devotees raised their war song and sauntered towards the shrine from all directions. The air was filled with their chant:

Ilotu wa ghwo
kokoya
oro vwe omo
se omo bruche
ma rhire

Under spell of their god and with fire in their eyes, Egba worshipers chased away the evangelizing bishop and his fanatical followers. The self-named bishop of the universe barely escaped lynching by being spirited away in a luxurious Toyota Land Cruiser, abandoning his entourage to their fates. His army inevitably scattered once the general escaped. The stragglers were beaten before being released to go and join their exorcist leader.

Since it is no longer modern to be members of traditional religious sects as *Igbe*, many folks leave such groups and become Christians. Some leaders of the Igbe sect have transformed themselves into Christians and now head new churches, many of which retain properties of juju sects. I call them juju churches where the pastors or evangelists use traditional religious methods and means to run their churches. They have the same types of mystical powers as traditional medicine men. They perform rituals to enhance their appeal to their congregations. Some have sweet tongues that make whatever they say sweet and acceptable to their congregations. I understand that many pastors go to medicine men for medicines or charms to hold their audiences enraptured. I have heard of rituals in which humans, babies, or human skulls are buried in the foundations of the churches when under construction or in some sacred spot inside or outside the church when already built. And such churches attract very large congregations, they say. Some pastors are said to serve Mami Wata; others have pythons in hidden pools that they invoke to perform miracles on their behalf. I don't really know whom our people serve today, the Almighty or Satan that their men of god invoke to perform healing miracles or ask for prosperity. There are different types of pastors, I found out during the period.

There are so many churches where I live in Effurun. My Ubuara Close stretches off All Saints Road that runs off Jefia Avenue. It is a fairly quiet area as far as residential areas are concerned in Effurun. It stands in sharp contrast to the Village, which is a slum part of Effurun adjacent to Jefia Avenue. Chief Jefia had bought hundreds of acres from Uvwie indigenes and partitioned the vast land into plots that outsiders bought to build houses. The quietness of the residents is countered by the noisy churches around. Wherever you turn to, there is one church or another. Sometimes their names are weird. But they range from Anglican Communion of Nigeria, Pan-African Church, the New Age Church, Mountain of Fire and Miracles, to Destiny Ministry, Rich Fate Ministries Incorporated, Redeem Church of Christ, Celestial Church of Christ, and Peculiar Generation.

My people are haunted by two troubling things: witchcraft and poverty. Often the two go together. They feel insecure spiritually and want to clutch to some mystical power they can hang on to without falling into the dark abyss. They feel insecure economically but nurse hope of wealth and want miracles to transform them into rich men and women. Really they don't care how this transformation from their niggardly condition to affluence comes about. But with so many pastors promising prosperity ahead of them, they go deep into the trance believing they would come out rich. Only miracles can solve these problems because they lack the sanity and knowledge to be healthy and they are so poor without the education and training to rise to earn living wages. The result is to make the pastor the god to bring security and prosperity.

Pentecostalism is spreading like wildfire and it appears it is unstoppable. The superstitions of the people and their precarious condition of poverty form the perfect soil for the growth of the new religions. If you believe that you are not safe in your own home, village, town, or family because witches are after you, how will you not seek refuge at the new spiritual advisers' churches? If you believe that others are keeping you down and so preventing you from being rich, how will you not join a church that promises you instant prosperity? If you are ignorant and ignore healthy habits and soon fall into a chronic ailment that you fear is terminal, how will you not go to church to not only perform a miracle cure but also save you from going to hell? And that is instead of going to the hospital to seek a cure.

Many of my people die for lack of knowledge. There is no public awareness of diseases. Even some of the doctors are as bad as the ignorant people. Maybe that is why the suffering people bypass them and go to the pastors for deliverance. A friend in the United States tells me that the average African in the First World with much public health enlightenment knew much about health than many of the doctors graduating from some universities with teaching hospitals in Nigeria. I now agree with him. I was in a company of men discussing diabetes. One of the men who talked as if he knew so much said that hypertension and diabetes always go together. I told him that was not always true, but he questioned what knowledge I had to disprove him. I told him there were many diabetics without hypertension and he was talking to one without knowing and he had no hypertension! At another function at Sapele, the talk went again to diabetes, an epidemic in the land. The doctor said that diabetics die about six years after being diagnosed. Wrong, dead wrong, I knew but shut my mouth. Sometimes one leaves ignorance to shame itself. The point about all these anecdotes is that the generality of the populace is superstitious, ignorant, poor, and diseased, and so with many incompetent doctors and uncaring state governments now resorts to the men of god who promise miracles for prosperity and prescribe anointed water to cure every disease from chronic headaches, glaucoma, AIDS, to anything distressing.

Every day in Effurun is filled with religious practice of one form or another. A typical Effurun/Warri day starts with morning calls in the street: *"Who dey run from church to church na ashewo."* Sunday, as in many places in Nigeria, is a busy day for my people to show their devotion to Christianity. The talk of town is that everybody is now a Christian. But this is a cynical statement and not a positive one. Many Nigerians now feel ashamed to be seen as not being Christian (or Muslim) and so go to church to be seen as one. If Nigeria is so Christian, it would not be one of the most corrupt countries in the entire world. But religion in Nigeria has nothing to do with cleanliness at heart. But let me not pursue this too far so as not to be seen as judging my own people. Let me make two points before continuing on the rise of the pastoral class in contemporary Nigeria.

Many Christians are only Christians in name and do not have faith in God and their prayers to Him. They feel so insecure and helpless in so many ways that they want to make juju stuff but are ashamed of going to the traditional medicine man. So, they go to the pastor in the church to provide them protection; hence they seek miracles. They don't seem to be interested in the Word of God or the Bible per se but go to the pastor for what they seek. They do not believe in their own ability to reach the Almighty and so go to the pastor or priest, the only way they think they can get to God. They are outsourcing their tasks to the pastor! With this, the pastor assumes so much importance irrespective of the motive of his or her pastoralism.

I heard of a resident of my Jefia neighborhood. Though a graduate, he refused to teach and so remained unemployed for more than seven years after graduation. He woke up one dreary raining season day and proclaimed to those in the compound where he had rented an apartment that from thenceforth he was going to be a man of god. He had got a vision at night and he was told by God to minister to his people. He assumed a new piety that he deemed fitted the pastoral mission he was setting out to live. The man's teacher wife had been running the house with her pay. She paid the rent of their apartment, paid the children's fees in private schools, and provided for the house. Within a year, the niggardly dressing man who had woken from a vision to be a pastor now wore Italian shoes, Gucci watches, had Gucci cologne, and designer suits. According to the story, he was among the first to pay his rent which used to accumulate for almost two years. He had been transformed as Pastor and both he and his wife are Daddy and Mommy of the Church! He seems to lack nothing basic but he tells people now that he needed a jet plane like other top pastors in the country crisscrossing the land officiating at ceremonies.

Pastors preside over social and cultural events. They have usurped the position of elders, traditional leaders and rulers, and others to be in control of everything happening. They have succeeded in creating a mystique around themselves in order to lead and exploit superstitious people living precarious lives. In fact, they take control of everybody and everything. They now fix marriages for members of their congregations. Once they hear about anything about you, they invite you to see them. Mind you, they call you to see them. They invited a chap who was involved in an accident and though the uninsured car was a write-off, he escaped unscathed. The pastor told him he needed a thanksgiving service. Here was somebody who had not recovered from the shock of the accident and was distraught about how to get a new car to replace the wrecked one being asked for a thanksgiving in which he would give money and other gifts to the pastor and treat fellow members of the congregation with food and drinks! A university lecturer was kidnaped and was released after a ransom which his church did not contribute to. Once released, his pastor assumed he should be in control of his life because of the miracle performed for his not being harmed when kidnaped. The survivor of the kidnaping and I were involved in an argument. I told him my attitude to thanksgiving. One's own personal communion with the Almighty is more intimate than what somebody else, pastor or intercessor, can do. I told him if he had money he should take a vacation for at least a week or ten days and heal from the psychological ordeal. However, the lecturer spoke passionately about the power of prayers that the pastor coordinated and told me that their prayers might have led to his safe release because there have been instances in which ransoms were paid and the kidnaped person still died. To him, "paying the ransom was not everything." I nodded respectfully to his counter argument.

I am always amused when I see pastors or whatever name they call themselves at the high table with bottles of wine, plates of kola nuts, fried meat and fish, bowls of rice or traditional foods set on their tables as they sit contented in their pastoral duties of men of god. It is my opinion that spending money on thanksgiving to pastors or paying tithes or other monies to pastors is based on ignorance. I would feel that helping my neighbors or the needy in my community will be a better way of serving God than enriching those who arrogantly call themselves men of god. Humans should serve God and not pastors by any name they assume or call themselves.

Human beings are prone to foibles whether they are ordinary human beings or men of god. There are too many pastor stories which relate to money-making or sexual scandals. Other human beings are also involved in such scandals but being ordinary humans makes them less talked about. The searchlight shines on those who call themselves men of god and, by the expectation of their vocation, ought to be exemplary figures.

A fake pastor who was arrested for demanding two hundred thousand naira from one who needed prayers and healing defended himself by saying that he needed the money for spiritual communication! I also heard of a pastor who ministered to a member of his congregation with a problem and made him give up his huge deep freezer for selling drinks to him and he installed it in his own shop! Another pastor, knowing his congregation member who was rich was seriously sick asked him to dispose of his material wealth to be well. The sick rich man, afraid he would die without listening to his pastor, brought out his cache of coral beads and gold and gave to the pastor. Fortunately the sick man's wife was witness to what transpired. The man died some days later and the pastor refused to give back to the deceased's wife the beads and gold he had extracted from a dying man. A junior colleague I mentor stopped going to his church when the pastor who watched what his congregation put in the huge basket near the altar as offering told him that he knew what he earned as a senior lecturer in the university and so should put enough as his offering! The same pastor of the same church that my colleague used to attend said the man of god spent over three quarters of the time to preach about tithes and the remaining time on church projects rather than anything from the Bible. He even cursed folks: "God will send to damnation whoever lies in the paying of tithes. God sees all of you and if you hide anything from Him by not paying your full tithe, you are surely going to hell!"

The pastors have healing or anointing water or oil for members of their congregation and others to drink, bathe with, or use as necessary to heal themselves. Followers of one pastor say that there is no disease on earth he cannot cure. I found that scandalous to say in these days of modern science that there is no disease that a specific pastor cannot cure. These pastors have become charlatans boasting of curing every disease on earth which is a big joke and lie. They have made their followers to believe they cannot have a wholesome and safe life without using what they give them. The congregation members need to fast, come for all-night vigil the last Friday of the month, and so on. I have seen a wife's friend disobeying her husband over attending an all-night vigil and saying she was ready to leave her marriage and continue going to the all-night activities in the church. The divorce took place and scandals broke out months later. Not about my friend's former wife but with some other women having liaisons with a junior pastor during the all-night vigil! The choruses of alleluias might be covering love moans.

Something amuses me in a very cynical manner about many new churches. I saw this on television and the few times I followed friends out of politeness to church. The testimonies have opened me to see Nigeria more as a land of spirits. Many result from acts of the pastors of the big new churches. The period of testimonies is one of the most bewildering times in any service. Nigerians have generally become so religious (but not moral or ethical). Everything ends with "We thank God!" There are many now greeting you with "God bless you!" I am not surprised that Warri boys and girls ask to be "blessed." I tell them that "Only God blesses one!" But let me come back to deliverances. Life has become so dire and precarious that miracles for which one should be thankful to God and so make public testimonies in the church are many. There are so many testimonies about escaping death in road accidents. After such a public avowal for being saved from Satan's grip, thanksgiving eventually follows. Nobody chastises the government for not making good roads available for cars to ply. No one wants regulations set up to check cars and buses to be in good condition before being on the roads. Nobody cries against the policemen on the road at checkpoints taking money instead of doing their duty. More accidents will take place and the survivors will go to their churches for thanksgiving. The victims of the accidents will be buried and forgotten. People see evil forces always on their trail.

At a bishop of the major new churches' crusade in Port Harcourt, one of those testifying to God's grace said: "I have been looking for American visa for over ten years and, Daddy, I got it!" A visa to America to clean toilets or stay for years without any job and be depressed! Another came up: "My son left for America twenty years ago. I wrote many letters but no response. I have been fasting and praying for years and years. Last week he sent me three hundred dollars by Western Union. Daddy, this is a miracle that my son has now written me and sent me dollars!" A university teacher was on the line of those giving testimonies. "I have been due for promotion from Lecturer I for over seven years. My enemies blocked it. Last week I got the letter from the Registrar of promotion to Senior Lecturer. Praise the Lord!" The congregation rebounded with shouts of "Alleluia!"

Many of the churches have their own television stations or networks where their services are relayed twenty-four hours every day. Their transmission is so powerful that they are streamed in the Internet within and outside the country. Their television networks are stronger than the Nigerian Television Authority stations. In the effort to win more converts, they highlight services with miracles and testimonies from Nigerians and non-Nigerians—Americans, South Africans, English, South Koreans, and so many others. Since many sick people are no longer taken to the hospital for treatment, they are taken to pastors to heal with anointed or healing water. It is a very theatrical scene, the deliverance process. It is almost the same among the big churches' pastors or whatever designation they bear. They stretch their hands towards the patient in the manner Jesus Christ did and later push him or her backwards. Many times the patients or the ones seeking deliverance fall on their own and act as if possessed by some spirit. The "healed" patients then stand up and are paraded for the congregation and the world to see the power of a pastor who can cure every disease! Some investigative journalists have traced some so-called healed people to the offices of the pastors themselves to confirm some pre-arranged deal. But I am not saying that all the performed miracles shown on churches' televisions are fake theatrics. I don't really know but my point is that there are so many cripples, blind folks, and severely sick in the streets in Lagos and elsewhere in the country but those ones are never the ones healed. I have asked some die-hard supporters of some pastors and bishops and all they tell me is that if I watch their church television, I would see what is happening. "After all," I am often told, "people come from South Africa, America, and England to seek deliverance and be healed!"

Many testimonies I have heard of or watched on television have to do with spiritual husbands of beautiful women. It is such a common phenomenon from the testimonies. The women having spiritual husbands still marry mundane men. One of such stories speaks of the spiritual husband at night coming to sleep between the woman and her earthly husband on the same bed. The man testifying said he saw the spirit husband. At a time the spiritual husband came to take the woman away.

"You can't take her away; she is my wife," the earthly husband shouted.

"She is mine and I am taking her away," the spiritual one told his earth rival.

The spiritual man wanted to take the woman away through the ceiling and roof of the house and held her by the head. The earth rival held tightly to her legs.

"Leave my wife for me," the spiritual man told his rival.

"No, she is my wife. Leave my wife for me," the earth man countered.

And the war of words and the tug of war continued. Each man summoned the resources of his manhood, the spiritual with invisible forces and the human with all the energy at his disposal. Then the earth man started to shout.

"Leave my wife for me-o!"

The shout woke neighbors, who thought the man and his wife were fighting at night, presumably over sex. There were knocks at the door. With the loud knocks, the spirit husband let go the head of his wife and she and her human husband fell on the bed! The earth man opened the door and told the men gathering at his door that he was fine. They must have left thinking of the woman rethinking and agreeing to sex with her man than anything else.

But at the testimony, the man said his wife had been delivered and he had not seen his wife's spiritual husband, his rival, come again to sleep between him and her. And not to talk of his rival trying to take away the woman he had paid a heavy bride price on and married in the church! "Alleluia!" the church thundered.

There are many testimonies by men and women who find it difficult to have children but after coming to the church they start to have babies. This is also a common phenomenon. Maybe the woman has blood clots and she cannot carry pregnancy to term or the man has wax or kerosene sperm (or low sperm count) that is incapable of impregnating a woman. Often the pastors pray for them and they come back to give testimonies and do thanksgiving for the miracle performed. One sees almost postmenopausal women dancing with babies. In Warri, I hear of the "Port Harcourt babies." It appears some women finding it difficult to conceive travel out and get pumped up with some contrivance as if pregnant. After a while they return to the "child clinic" somewhere in the Port Harcourt area to be delivered. Such women later come back to their homes with babies. After the discovery of so many baby factories in the south east and south-south geopolitical zones, one has to be cynical about babies that do not look in any way in complexion and physical shape like their mothers or fathers! Of course, such "mothers" would go for thanksgiving.

Another phenomenon often testified about has to do with marine spirits. I have from childhood heard of "Emete r'ame," literally water girls, in the Urhobo area. But the phenomenon spreads across the Niger Delta region. Women often come to be delivered of this spirit that possesses them. They are queens underwater and are committed to mischief.

Many of such women are said to be fair and beautiful and often compared to Mami Wata, the water goddess. The women under the spell of marine spirits often behave unpredictably and suffer mood swings. They don't seem to be sociable or good wives or partners because of being constantly under the spell of the invisible but powerful spirit. A friend has told me of how he could not sleep with his girlfriend during the night when she was, while asleep, constantly talking a weird language with an invisible male figure. He only made love with her during the day. That must be a marine spirit-possessed woman, I now think. Once they are brought to the pastors, they are delivered in a simple rite. After this, they become normal, according to the claims.

I have an observation about many of the deliverances done by some of these church leaders and their lieutenants. One person testified of an "Internet spirit" harassing her. Others talk of hearing voices giving orders on what they should do. Many others confess they are witches. And so the men of god cast out demons and deliver those who come to them from evil spirits. In fact, some pastors charge heavily for strong cases of these spiritual problems because they complain they are risking their own lives in trying to deliver their clients of strong evil spirits.

Who am I to talk of conmen in these matters? We are all human and prone to foibles. However, I strongly believe that many of these sick folks said to be possessed by evil spirits are suffering from psychiatric, neurotic, or psychological and mental problems. Many are suffering from either bipolar or unipolar types of depression; hence they are said to be possessed by demons that command them to hurt themselves or others. I have heard of someone eating sand or mud; others eating grass. Are these people not crazy? Or can we say that any mental case is one of a demonic possession? Those having deep mood swings are suffering from clinical depression. I think those who take their relatives or friends to these churches for deliverance should try their luck with hospitals first for medical diagnoses of the patients. It is when the medical doctors fail that they could try the men of god who seem not to have the knowledge to treat them but have the power to deliver them from those "spirits" as a temporary relief. Yes, temporary because I have heard of some persons said to be delivered of diabetes and hypertension and they believed, only for them to die a few months later from stroke or heart attack.

It is an anomaly for rich pastors or bishops with planes to minister to the poor. The Christian ministers should come to the level of those they minister to. They should be modest or poor and not just preach prosperity to folks that have no resources or training to be ever become prosperous. They should not promise cures to sick or disabled people they cannot cure and when they fail, they blame the patients for not having enough faith! Miracles don't come easy even among the old prophets. In fact, a friend of mine told me that Jesus Christ did not perform miracles every day or every week; he performed only several miracles all his lifetime.

I hear masses of people beginning to question the affluence and opulence of their men of god. A barrister friend of mine who goes to a Catholic church speaks of the priest of his church having three cars, including a Toyota Sequoia and a brand-new Mercedes. He is living a good life and there are rumors that reverend fathers are now building houses for their parents in their hometowns. This father insists on many offerings, another name for collections, at each Mass. He is not accountable to anybody and spends the church's money as he pleases. A female friend tells me the same of the Anglican Communion of Nigeria where the Venerable reinvents ways to collect money. There are now so many types of thanksgiving, including the family, individual, and general thanksgivings, two of which now take place in a year. In addition, there are children and adult bazaars, half-year harvest, children's harvest, adult harvest, and countless requests for donations for projects. A woman relative told me of her African Church where "The pastor collects money too much." What is meant to be voluntary is now mandatory. Almost all the churches now use a form of blackmail and coercion to raise money. One has to stand and walk to the altar to put money in the collection basin under the wide stare of the priest or pastor. Some pastors go as far as telling the congregation that nobody should drop anything less than one hundred naira into the collection bucket; a few say at least two hundred.

Many pastors and reverend fathers now ask their congregation to "sow seeds" that will grow into prosperity. By this, they mean that one should give to God (whom they represent and on whose behalf they keep the money) and they will be blessed in multiple ways. I have a cousin-in-law who retired from the civil service and had withdrawn part of her retirement emoluments home to think of what to do to supplement her income which was bound to be smaller than when she was working. That is, after going through the Camel's Eye to have the state start paying the pension. She lived with her only son. Coming home, the widow discovered that the one hundred thousand naira she kept in a drawer was gone. She sat her son down.

"Only you and I live in this house. Is it so?"

"Yes, Mommy!"

"I just wanted to be sure that there is no invisible person or spirit living with us," she said.

"We are only two," her twenty four-year old son replied.

He graduated three years earlier and had completed the national service. He has been at home for two years looking for a job with his degree in Industrial Mathematics.

"I am your mother. Tell me the truth! I kept one hundred thousand naira in the drawer in my bedroom and I can't see it. Did you take it?" she asked.

"I don't understand," he replied.

"Don't let me curse the person who stole my money!" she threatened.

Her son stood up, as if he wanted to walk out. The mother held him down.

"You are not going anywhere. Did you take the money?"

"OK, I took it to sow seeds. The priest asked us to sow seeds and I had to take it," he admitted.

"Take me to that priest and let me get back my money!" she ordered.

"I don't know whether he will give back the money," he said lamely.

"No, he must give me my money or I will raise hell in his church," she said.

Roland led his mother to the priest. From the anger he saw on the face of his congregation member's mother, Father Bernard knew there was trouble.

"Give me my one hundred thousand naira!" she ordered the priest.

"Are you encouraging stealing in your church? How do you expect an unemployed young man to have that sum of money and give it to you and say he is sowing seeds? What seeds is he sowing? Give me my money and let me go back to my home quietly!"

The priest went into his inner room and came back with a bundle of crispy thousand naira notes of one hundred thousand. Mother and son returned home without talking.

"No wonder a bank worker stole millions and gave to his church and he is now serving a long prison term," the mother told her son when they arrived home.

"The pastor of that church ought to serve the prison terms with him," the mother added.

"I am sorry, Mommy. I won't do that again!"

"Better change and not do that because the next time this type of thing happens, you and your reverend father will go to prison to reap the seeds of theft both of you sowed," the mother told her son.

A pastor of a church wanted to go on a pilgrimage to Jerusalem and asked his congregation to contribute the projected expenses for himself and his wife. The members of the congregation, overwhelmingly women, contributed twenty-thousand naira each, but that did not make a dent on the projected expenses of one and a half million naira. The pastor asked them whether there was some other money they could borrow from. The women had two million in their account and had to withdraw one million to support the pastor and his wife's pilgrimage to Jerusalem. They did not need to be told that that loan would never be repaid.

From the look of things, as I experienced while in Nigeria from May 2013 to June 2014, many who used to be blind to antics of the rich pastors and priests are now gradually waking up from the delirium and the spell cast on them. Members of congregations who have been subjected to extortion that has become the order of the day in church collections are grumbling out; sometimes loudly about too many collections and tithes. They see and complain too about the men of god living too lavishly at their expense. Rather reflective of the state of things at the time, a sister-in-law of mine took a praise-name, which underscores the exasperation with the tactics of the men and women of god. When called "Ishoshi akpona" (Present-day churches), she responds "Eki aye avwaye chua!" (They are business enterprises!). That is her perception and of so many others. If this trend went on, the churches would lose many of their congregations and the pastors, Papas and Mamas of their respective units incorporated, would have their stocks dip very low or even crash. If less attention is not paid to money from the congregation to an unaccountable clergy, there is bound to be a revolt someday and that will be awful for the churches.

Many churches are now building universities. Many will argue that the orthodox churches such as Catholic, Anglican, and Baptist, after all, have always had secondary schools and the students paid school fees. However, the objective is for low income earners and members of their church to send their children to these schools with fees lower than government schools. Today, there is hardly any government-owned or private university that charges higher fees than some universities owned by the new churches. I heard that over eighty percent of the church members can't afford to send their kids to the universities they all, in one way or another, contribute to support.

I see a dangerous phenomenon in Nigeria—the rise of many cults that are called churches. The Dictionary meaning of a cult involves "a system of religious veneration and devotion directed toward a particular figure" and "a misplaced or excessive admiration for a particular person." Many appear to be worshiping personalities rather than God. They so revere the pastors that they flare up whenever any objective criticism of their leader is done, even if supported by facts. They have outlandish beliefs about miracles and appear to be living in a fantasy world. They have blind faith in their pastors that they don't have in Christ or God! If nothing is done to stop or temper the fanaticism, many Nigerians will be zombies and mad folks filling up buildings on Sundays and worshiping pastors but not God. Can you imagine that members of some churches now call on the God of their leader? There are now God of this pastor, God of that pastor, God of this bishop, God of that bishop, God of this evangelist, God of that evangelist, and so many other Gods! Mind you, not many gods. It is a new development that the congregations now believe that the founders of their churches incorporated have their separate Gods.

Let me conclude with remarks about another new development—intercessors. They might have always been there but not publicized. They might have been there but faceless and really doing their work without drawing attention to themselves. But in the Nigeria of today, especially in the Delta, folks like publicity. Being known as an intercessor, many believe, would give them more assignments. So, a late friend's wife visited me and I asked about her friend, a woman I knew she had been friends with for decades.

"She is there-o. She has emaciated and looks sickly because of this her intercessor thing," she told me.

"What's an intercessor?" I asked.

"Those people who pray for other people," she explained.

I wanted to know more about this phenomenon. I knew all along that people solicit friends, relatives, and others to pray for them but still prayed for themselves. Now the person who wants prayers does not pray or have faith in his or her prayer and so gets somebody to do the praying for him or her. But what has sprung up lately is a group of self-appointed intercessors who feel and make others believe they are holy or spiritually pure enough to pray for others who are not as clean as themselves spiritually. Theresa was slim normally and did not look strong. She was also aging and had retired from teaching at sixty. I could imagine her austere look now that she had become a popular intercessor. Theresa fasts and prays for people. She does dry fasting, I learnt.

"She prays almost all night," I was told.

"When does she sleep then?"

"During the day!"

"She's now a rabbit, working at night and sleeping at daytime," I said.

"I have advised her that she is taking this intercession too far-o."

"How does she take care of herself?" I asked.

"She tells those she fasts and prays for to donate what they feel like giving out," she explained.

"And is that not payment?" I again asked.

"She says she does not want payment but some type of offering thing," she further explained.

There are so many problems in the land. The problems that beleaguer the folks are so ponderous that they look for ways to lighten the burden of life. That is why intercession has become a profession. The Nurse who testifies to the last days of the deceased and the professional mourner who grunts at burials of folks he does not know in South Africa came to my mind. Yes, Zakes Mda has portrayed such bizarre characters and the many ways of dying during the last days of apartheid and black-on-black violence in South Africa. With so many problems which are beyond the understanding of the sufferers and victims, the pastors and intercessors have to be summoned to fend off the satanic spirits. I see folks outsourcing fasting and praying to a professional. While I believe that others can pray for one, I also believe that I can best pray to God to assist me. But so bemused about Theresa's fame as an intercessor, I can imagine somebody making an offering to her to pray for him. She would be fasting and praying all night and becoming gaunt while the person she is interceding for is partying!

From my experience in the new churches whose services I attended, the pastors no longer preach the gospel of salvation or redemption of one's soul. Rather, it is almost all about prosperity or being protected from diabolic enemies. They tell the congregation that there is God. They also say hell is real but act as if their followers do not need to be shown how to live right and thus prepare for the second coming of Jesus that Christianity is supposed to be about. While I cannot judge others, it appears shepherds have lost sight of the core values of Christianity. Things have to change if the people have to be good citizens of the country.

5

SPIRITUAL ATTACK

Perhaps the most chilling word I heard during my more than one-year stay in Nigeria, especially in Effurun, is "Attack." It carried a heavy weight and was sharp at the same time. It was poisonous, often deadly. It flew out of mouths with such abandon that I wondered how such a terrible and terrifying word came out so easily. It was the deadliest weapon in the witches' arsenal and so honed in their covens that it had become omnipresent and omnipotent. That is, for those who believe in it and use it. Who am I to say that the word was used flippantly? I had been visiting Nigeria for over twenty-five years, sometimes thrice a year but for short intervals of two or few weeks, but no time before now had I been so publicly harangued by the spiritual attack of malicious and malevolent folks.

There was almost universal belief in it in the land. In a teeming land, I could not see a doubting Thomas even among the academics, priests and pastors, or the elders. Everybody had to be careful, often brace themselves for it and believe that some spiritual strength through the pastor's prayers or the medicine man's charms would be their shield. The attack is insidious, secretive, but believed to be effective. Only those who had effective *okpofia* or *orhakpo*, mystical deflectors, escaped it. Or those fortified spiritually or diabolically. To the residents of my homeland, it takes power to fight back power! And some types of powers are stronger than others; it was something I learnt from the common Pidgin English saying: "Power pass power." Also "Man pass man." Those who can "attack" are often more deadly than other powers. Each person attempts to secure an iron dome to avoid being hit. That iron dome is often installed in the body by medicine men or prayers. One should not expose oneself unnecessarily in the land, I learnt.

The "attack" was not of malaria and typhoid, common twin diseases rampant in the land. One is often misdiagnosed for the other but that did not make them as feared as the real "attack." It was not physical like something that had always been there since my secondary school days at Enerhe Junction with "tie neck" or at Effurun Market with physical assault and purse-snatching by weed-smoking Area Boys. People feared the daredevil youth often on drugs and could kill if you did not surrender your purse or bag. But the fear of "attack" was deeper than the fear of gangsters. It was not what the stranger would see as an attack. It is for the knowing homeboys who fear or use it. They pronounce it as a verdict after their mental diagnosis of the problem. It is instant judgment. The result of the attack could be sickness, poverty, accident, or some bad fortune. Nothing is seen as natural. There is no room for accidents in the homeland where every happening has been precipitated by malicious ones. No sickness or death is natural. Every negative thing comes down to "spiritual attack."

I had been introduced to a barber in my street. I then abandoned the one I was using in Ovie Palace Road that I paid five hundred naira instead of the normal three hundred each time I went to him. I even invited him to my house once to cut my hair and a friend's. We gave him one thousand three hundred naira. However, I had an appointment with him and he missed it without calling. Whenever he was to call me, he would "flash" me instead of calling me for a minute or two which would not cost him more than forty naira. As a rule, unless the call is from my mother, I don't call back when I am "flashed." I believe whoever really wants to speak to me will spend a minute or half minute to tell me he or she has no credit. So, I found Lucky's ploy of flashing instead of calling me unacceptable. Why can't someone I pay more than normal not spend forty naira or less to tell me something briefly? I had to leave him for Jerry in my street. I walk to Jerry and it takes me five minutes to get to his salon, unlike fifteen or more minutes to drive to Lucky's. And, until you try another, you never know. Jerry did a far better job than the "flashing" barber because each time he cut my hair, I received great compliments.

I like the barber's shop for the gossip and the behavior of our young folks. The television was always tuned to some foreign, usually English Premier League or some UEFA league soccer matches. The boys and men who came for haircut knew the names of the players to the last and knew the history and everything about the teams and their managers. I am sure they did not care about Nigerian players in Nigeria but followed thoroughly the careers of Nigerian players in foreign leagues. Once in a while I asked Jerry questions about Effurun and Warri and we started to be familiar and to engage in a conversation during the twenty-five minutes or so that he spent in cutting my hair.

Then came some time I wanted to cut my hair and he was not around. I had taken his phone number to be sure that I went to his salon and not have an unnecessary walk at night. I did most of my hair cutting in the late evening or early night— about seven o'clock.

"Jerry, when are you coming next to the salon?"

"Not today, sir. Maybe I'll come tomorrow. I have bereavement," he told me.

"Sorry-o," I told him as a sort of condolence.

"When I am there, I will call you," he told me.

I waited three days and called him again.

"I will be there this night," he said.

"OK, I will come."

I walked with my haircutting kit to Jerry's salon. He was the "master" of the salon and had several boys working under him. They must have an arrangement which I did not quite understand but it appeared that in a society where cheating is taken as normal, he wanted to curtail it. Every chap cutting hair had to write down something to register the number of haircuts for that day, I suppose. Jerry got his fee from each haircut done by his assistants.

When I arrived, Jerry was not there. I called to tell him that I was already there waiting for him.

"I will be there in another five minutes," he assured me.

Twenty minutes later he was still not around. I then decided to allow any of his boys to cut my hair. After all, my hair was not bushy. I just wanted it to be neater and have that well-groomed appearance. When one of the boys had a vacant chair, he beckoned on me to come. I went to sit down for the haircut. As he arranged his tools, tying a shawl over my neck, my phone rang.

"Where are you?" It was Jerry.

"I am already seated. Come in and do it."

His boy left me for him.

"What's wrong all these days that you have not been coming to work?" I asked.

"I lost my daughter."

"Oh no! Sorry-o!" I told him.

"She just died like that," he further told me.

"What sickness killed her, malaria, typhoid or what?" I asked, cataloguing the child-killers that roamed the land.

"No, sir, it was an attack!" he told me.

In Nigeria parents may not be aware of Sudden Infant Death (SID) syndrome and whatever took a baby's life in a land where infant mortality is extremely high is taken as an "attack." To Jerry, it was not a natural sickness that took his baby daughter's life. Rather, it was some witch jealous of a barber and his wife who used mystical weapons to eliminate the daughter by snuffing her life.

A popular Isoko masseur and his assistants had been strongly recommended to me as the ones who could massage my daughter's legs to make them supple enough to regain good circulation that would make her walk. The Anis, who knew the masseur, and I decided on a date to see him and arrange for my daughter's treatment to begin. Early in the morning, the Anis in front in their own car, I and my wife following in our car, drove to Orhughworun where the famed Isoko masseur and spiritualist attended to people with displaced or broken bone, leg, or hand problems. When we arrived at where he used to be, he had relocated to Orhoakpor or somewhere after some altercation with the community. We were disappointed that the masseur's hall was deserted. As we were about to turn back, the Anis saw one of the masseur's trusted and able lieutenants. The assistant also saw Mrs. Ani that he had attended to and so stopped.

Mrs. Ani had been involved in a ghastly bus accident and every August, about the time of the accident, the initial pains in her legs at the time of the accident resurfaced. It was the Isoko masseur and Emmanuel that had attended to her. From the look of things, she had relief from the acute pain and she believed these men could help my daughter. We felt relieved that though we missed the chief masseur, his trusted assistant, Emmanuel, was around to help us with my daughter's problem. Emmanuel said he had to take us to his residence in Ekrokpe, since we needed to know where he lived. He would later explain that after the communal clash that involved his master, the Isoko man had moved to Orhoakpor while he relocated to nearby Ekrokpe.

Ekrokpe Village was close to Ekakpamre, the hometown of my wife, Anne. I found it interesting that Emmanuel lived in Ekrokpe that suffered the butt of Okitiakpe's *udje* songs. Ekrokpe that was too close to Ekakpamre to take a walk to with a lover! Ekrokpe of the tongue-twisting *Kua kpe Ekrokpe, Kua kpe Ekrokpe, Ekrokpe be ekuara!* Pack and go to Ekrokpe, pack and leave for Ekrokpe, Ekrokpe is not far to get to! What a pity the English translation doesn't twist the tongue as the Urhobo version does!

Emma took us to his home. He introduced himself as Evangelist Emma. We discussed with him and, because of the relatively short stay of Anne and Eloho in Nigeria, the Evangelist had to start work immediately. He promised to come to us in Effurun in the afternoon of the same day. We settled on an amount of money to be paid as his fees—one hundred and ten thousand naira.

At two o'clock he arrived. He kept to his word, and that gladdened my heart immensely. He saw Eloho, looked at her and then checked her legs.

"It is an attack!" he pronounced.

He would spend the next four weeks using herbs and massaging to remedy the negative effects of that "attack." Towards the end of Eloho's stay in Nigeria, he would recommend scents, powder, and some types of candles to be lit, as he prayed. He went after the physical spastic paralysis with herbs and massaging. He used snake oil and other types of oil to rub the legs and waists, after which he tied some herbs around the waist and the two legs. At night he confronted the spiritual powers with prayers and other forces and that was when he lit the candles overnight. There was some improvement in Eloho's limbs. While I attributed the improvement to the massaging and the herbs, no doubt the Evangelist without a church must be thinking he was fighting a spiritual attack with an offensive of his own!

It was not only ordinary people who talked of attacks or were attacked. University folks and priests and pastors also were attacked or saw attacks in people's conditions. These are two groups I had thought their respective intellectual capacity and faith in God would make them unique and not believe in spiritual attacks. But I was wrong on them. I came to Nigeria to teach and the University became my gateway to knowing about my people I had left for a long time.

I was in a junior colleague's office and a female student came in to be given a makeup test because she had traveled when the actual test took place.

"Why did you not come to take the test when I announced the time and date to everybody in the class," Dr. Amos asked.

"Sir, I lost my father. He just died suddenly," she explained.

"Sorry, Judith, I didn't know you lost your father," the lecturer said.

Judith broke into sobs.

"What killed him? Was he sick or what happened?"

"It was a spiritual attack!" she said.

I had been listening without saying a word but had to ask:

"How do you know he died of spiritual attack?"

"Our pastor said so," she explained.

I nodded my head in amazement. The pastor has become the doctor performing autopsy and announcing causes of death to members of his congregation. Up till now, I still wonder at the pastor's expertise at this. However, Judith says: "Our pastor said so."

Vice-Chancellors are academic emirs or *obas* to whom many members of the faculty and staff literally prostrate. They exercise executive dominion over the academy. From the lobbying that would land them at the VC's desk, a lot could be compromised in the process of exercising their duties. But that is by the way. One would expect a Vice-Chancellor though to be very educated and rational the way he or she looks at things. But some have come to be identified with either their spiritual fortifications or as victims of "attacks." A VC of a central Federal University tops the list of juju men in office in Nigeria. He must have assumed the office as one under threat and felt he had to spend his five years there fortifying himself, neutralizing attacks, and amassing wealth. Bizarre stories accompany him. He had been seen at night, according to some professors, half-naked at the intersection that led to his campus chanting and murmuring things. The same VC was said to make sure that he saw the food served at Senate meetings and the rumor went that he sprinkled some powdery substances on the food. For what purpose nobody knows exactly but maybe to make zombies of his senior academic staff who would always concur with whatever he said or did. Despite the spiritual fortifications, strikes almost consumed his entire tenure as VC and he left with a legacy of not achieving anything in the infrastructure of the university or academic development. He was just part of the statistics of VCs of that jinxed university. Of course, his resume would list his years of Vice Chancellorship and that would bring him a political appointment, if he used part of his largess from the University to support a political party that would give him a political appointment.

A VC of another federal university was flown overseas for medical treatment. Spiritual as his people were said to be in the Mami Wata cult, they could not treat him. When I asked about him, the instant response was "He is under attack!" I did not think he returned from overseas before the process for the selection of another VC started. As of this time, I don't know his fate: whether or not he survived the attack or still battling it.

I visited one VC to congratulate him for his appointment. When I entered his office, he was drinking tea. The tea was creamy and there might be many cubes of sugar dissolved in it. He sipped the tea as we talked. He relished the sweetness of the tea, a metaphor for his office in which he could do what he wanted. The University was interviewing folks for so many positions and he came on break to attend to some things. He signed so many documents in my presence. Before signing one, he said "This man was one of those opposing me and supporting some other candidate for this position. I will still sign it for him. Now he must know that I am the boss!" It seemed he cancelled the amount of funds requested drastically to show that he was now in charge of things. He told me how he used an Ijo connection to lobby successfully for the position while the local Ovie was supporting a Hausa man who had given him plenty of cash.

"Don't let that influence your administration," I told him. "Let every group as long as qualified benefit from your tenure," I further advised.

"I will, but one does not forget easily," he said.

We shook hands as he had to go back to the interviews going on. I saw him lumbering rather clumsily and I felt if this man were of the same age with me then I must be far gone.

Barely four weeks later, I heard that he had been flown overseas for treatment because he was very sick. I was not too surprised because of the stress he must have gone through in lobbying for the position and being now overwhelmed by the governance of the place. A reverend father who had introduced me to him during my visit invited me, a neighbor, and another priest for dinner at a posh hotel in Effurun/Warri. It was an exclusive hotel I had never known though I style myself as a Wafi homeboy. Most of those in the hotel were expatriates who did not seem to go out after work but enjoyed the best luxuries around of food and women. We were having a good dinner with the priests taking beer and I taking red wine. The VC came into our conversation.

"The Chairman of Council and the Registrar have taken over the activities of the VC. The Council and Senate have awarded all the contracts for all the jobs that need to be done in the next five or more years," the senior father said.

"What happened to our friend, the VC?" I asked.

"Attacked!" the two priests exclaimed.

It appears to them that the professor exhausted himself and his resources for nothing, if he was to fall sick at a time when he should be enjoying as boss of the place. None of my dinner companions thought about a pre-existing condition of an aging man. To them, it had to be an "attack." Pity the academic gown is no armor against "spiritual attacks." And it is a pity the cassock believes in spiritual attacks.

Pastors are also attacked. Jefia Avenue where I live has over twelve churches. If people in an area became holy because of the number of churches they have, Jefia Avenue residents would have been some of the holiest human beings in the world. I was a secular humanist, an infidel, though in the street of born-again fanatics. All the churches with weird and strange names were there. A new church, Glorious Moment International Ministry, started at the intersection of Jefia Avenue and All Saints Street. As often happens with such churches, it started with a congregation of four. It then grew to fifteen, and then twenty. Whenever I walked or drove past in the morning at about ten o'clock, I could hear the pastor's congregation clapping, singing, dancing, speaking in loud tongues. The pastor's voice always boomed. In it was divine authority that held his congregation spellbound. What was a temporary small building was brought down and within a week a long log house was built. In one of my morning walks, I had to enter the church premises to see it. The church was bigger inside than when seen from outside. The ramshackle outside appearance of a plank house belies its comfortable inside. It was rugged and fancifully decorated with flowers. Fans were installed at different parts of the church to prevent a hot and humid atmosphere. It was early morning and only the pastor and about three members of his congregation were there.

Wonder of wonders it was that this church grew within five weeks to full capacity. One Sunday, as I heard, Pastor Ezekiel delivered a sick person who had been poisoned by a close relative. He had named the people who had poisoned the woman and the woman was surprised that the man of god, her pastor, was so spiritually adept as to know her enemies. The same Sunday, he cast out demons from a young lady who said that she had been bewitched and prevented from having a husband by her aunt. Pastor Ezekiel was moderate in size and possessed a cool demeanor. However, when he saw evil spirits "attacking" members of his congregation, he seemed to be highly energized. Then he bounced from one end of the altar to the other. Sometimes he walked through the aisle gazing at people's eyes to see what was wrong with them. He spotted folks with problems and revealed them to astound them, as I heard.

Words spread fast that Pastor Ezekiel exorcized demons from troubled or sick members of his congregation. He even called names of witches to his congregation. He pointed at the very source of his church member's spiritual attack. Effurun and Warri men and women loved this type of priest who was fearless and knew those attacking members of his congregation. By the following Sunday, many cars parked along Jefia Avenue and the adjoining streets. Rich men and women heard and joined. They needed a strong pastor to protect them from jealous eyes in their family or community. They wanted a warrior pastor under whose shadow and power they could continue to increase their wealth and become even richer than they expected. They wanted to be invincible rich folks that no evil could "attack." They expected the pastor to be their divine shield against any attempt to either stop their increasing wealth or poison them.

A special deliverance service was announced for another Sunday. That day Pastor Ezekiel was in his elements, as the story went, and he "caught" many witches in his church.

He named witches tormenting members of his congregation. He was a pastor with invisible eyes that saw whatever happened anywhere a member of his congregation lived. He appeared omnipresent himself and his revelation of misdeeds and evil deeds of those there mystified his congregation. His eyes lit with brightness that seemed to penetrate the body to see through people's minds and souls. He could see what the future held for those before him. He saw those whose future wealth was already being squandered by relatives who were witches. With prayers and fasting he could keep such people's future wealth intact for them to achieve. He could see those whose good health was being undermined by satanic forces. He would recommend prayers and fasting to such people to retain their God-given good health.

"Nobody will snatch away your health!"

"Amen!" folks would chorus.

One expected the Sunday after that to have the Church spilling over into the streets. By word of mouth, friends and relatives of those that attended the previous Sunday prepared to worship at Pastor Ezekiel's church. The expectations were high. Pastors of nearby churches wondered what was happening that was decreasing their congregations and increasing Pastor Ezekiel's church because they had noticed that many of their worshipers had cross-carpeted to the new church. The world was anxious to see what the next Sunday's service would bring.

But Pastor Ezekiel suddenly fell sick and was flown overseas. By the other Sunday he had died of an undiagnosed illness in London. Members of his congregation wept outside his church which was soon padlocked. "They attacked him!" the story went.

"He went too far to expose witches publicly and they of course took revenge to test his power. They attacked him and he did not survive," a neighbor told me.

I would not like to be attacked.

"Iboyi has become mental. It was an attack. His family of witches did it," a cousin informed me of my childhood friend in Ibada Village.

In the land there is no depression. Nothing is attached to the genes one inherits. Iboyi's first cousin on the maternal side had been mad and one is not allowed to link the two "attacks" as genetically engineered by their great-great-grandparents. Glaucoma was an attack. Diabetes and hypertension are attacks. So many impotent men around have been attacked because they had multiple wives or wicked family members. The word "cholesterol" does not show up in the Urhobo or other Nigerian languages. Prostate cancer, breast cancer, ovarian cancer, and hypertension were manifestations of "attacks." There is so much evil out there among ignorant people and their fears and consequences of uninformed lives turn into "attackers," initiated by witches and wizards!

There was a new source of "attack" among women while I was in Nigeria. Even educated women I knew confirmed it. In the company of a female university professor, I heard about the new brushfire of womanhood.

"Do you know I am always now on fire?" Prof. Aggy proclaimed.

"The same with me too-o! I no fit talk before-o," Dr. Rosy added humorously.

"My own na wild fire raging in the savannah," said Dr. Helen, who had got her Ph.D. in Geography from Ahmadu Bello University, Zaria, in the savannah region.

The women ranged from late forties to mid-fifties. They can be attacked by their breasts, vaginas, or their whole body set on fire. They could be attacked by the beast of irrationality without their knowing. They were educated, sophisticated, I would say. They knew so much about sex which they talked about without being coy about it. In fact, they shocked me with their sex language of using vibrators or other toys rather than sleeping with a man beneath their education or social rank. They unabashedly talked about sexual positions that I had never heard about before then. Some even demonstrated those positions to others, knowing fully well that a man was in their midst. Despite their immense knowledge in so many areas and dressed in decency, they cannot connect their apparent menopause that came to my mind to their being set on fire! They said they were not going to their village homes again because there could have been the source of their "attacks." I suspect the bare chested village women would not complain of their being set on fire by any "attacks."

I feel the worst "attacks" tearing down the lives of people in my homeland are superstition, ignorance, illiteracy, and fear.

6

ADDENDUM TO SPIRITUAL POWER: FAITH AS AN IRRATIONAL BEAST

After my stay in Nigeria for six months, my wife and two daughters came to visit me. It took some time for my wife to arrange a five-week leave to visit. She had to schedule it around my senior daughter who is wheelchair-bound and who receives transfusion every three months. My other daughter, Amreghe, fondly named after my Grandmother, Mother Hen, would fly on her own from Washington, DC, where she works through London Heathrow to meet us at Abuja and from where all of us would go to Delta State. Amreghe was of no interest to people around as Eloho who drew attention because of her being wheelchair-bound.

Earlier on, my late friend's wife, Mrs Queen Ewubare, was kind enough to drive to the Murtala Muhammed Airport to pick Anne and Eloho to her home in Lekki for the night before their trip to Warri the day after arrival. Anne and Queen remain good friends despite the distance between Nigeria and the United States. Even though a friend of mine and Anne's senior sister lived closer to the airport, she insisted on spending the night with her friend. After all, since my good friend, Joe, died, Anne had not had time to spend with her and talk except by phone. Anne does not have as much opportunities of visiting Nigeria frequently because of the nature of her work which will not allow her on leave for more than two weeks. She visits once in a while, maybe at four or five-year intervals. The following morning Queen would drive to take one of those transport lines and come to Warri. I had advised her to charter one Sienna minivan for the trip. My friend would make the arrangement and Queen would drop Anne and Eloho at his house in Jibowu, Yaba, for the direct trip to Warri.

So my friend saw Eloho for the first time. He had known all along I have a daughter who has been wheelchair-bound since she was about seven years old but never seen her till their joint trip in the same minivan to Warri. Eloho could not walk but could manage with a walker or metal cane at home. Often in a new environment, as the Nigerian one, it would be difficult for her to function properly. Of course, in Nigeria there is no such thing as the American Disability Act which requires every public space or utility to provide for the wheelchair-bound. That means there should be a ramp for wheelchairs to enter a building. Also the toilet rooms would be larger and have steel bars that normal restrooms don't have. For those who drive, there is space reserved for the disabled.

However, Nigeria has not woken up to the plight of those who are disabled or the physically challenged. In the United States, Eloho functions fairly well. There is a ramp not just to my house but to classrooms, theatre houses, shopping malls, every public space and utility. Special toilets are reserved for the physically challenged. Those mandated structural adjustments to spaces make life more convenient for the disabled. Those are in addition to Medicare which takes care of their health expenses. Many receive a monthly stipend to take care of their living expenses. So you can see Eloho's dilemma in a very different world, a new place. Or rather, she finds herself in a strange environment.

I can imagine her being stared at by everybody, which could have not only embarrassed her but also tormented her emotionally. A thirty-seven year old woman would hate that fate but she had managed it very well where folks understood that the disadvantaged in society through physical disability needed special state care. In the American home she felt all right, to put it that way, because she realized that bad as her condition was, she was better off than so many other physically handicapped people. She could take care of herself—she might be slow but she took care of herself. With the Nigerian public staring, I could imagine her embarrassed by what she did not cause to herself but due to an accident of fate. I think she has reconciled herself to her condition for now though always hoping for the better.

When they arrived at my house in Effurun, she had to come down last. Many stared at her. I saw the unceasing gaze as if she was a strange being from another planet. Efe, a neighbor's son, came to help, as Anne and I had to balance her to go up the stairs. I have no ramp where I live in Effurun to take her up on the wheelchair which has to be carried up with her. My friend who accompanied them played his part in assisting as much as he could under the circumstances. My friend who accompanied them from Lagos had some official assignment in the state and left after three days. As soon as he got back, he called.

"Tanure, you have to try some prayer therapy for your daughter. Hers was a spiritual attack. She took the bullet for you," he said.

"How did she take the bullet for me?" I asked.

"Something was meant for you but they couldn't get you and so turned to her and got her!"

I was surprised at the assurance of knowing so much about an aspect of me I did not even know. I knew he meant well. I had heard so much before about the cause of her suddenly losing her walking ability when she was nine. Some folks had said she had walked over a line drawn to cripple her or me or any member of my family. Others have told me and Anne that my wicked relatives, who must be witches, wanted to punish me because I so loved her as my first daughter. There are still some others who felt they knew why her legs had been "seized" to punish my wife. Only an ex-Federal Government College lady nurse at Maiduguri told me that what she had was spastic paralysis as a result of her sickling cells.

"There is a group of reverend fathers who do healing. They are gathered from across the country, especially the East, and they spend time in praying for cases as your daughter's. All you have to do is buy boxes of candles, pay their transportation to where they will convene, pay for their accommodation, and the money they will use in buying food to break their fast," my friend explained.

"How does that work?" I asked.

"It is easy," he replied. "They don't even need your daughter's physical presence but only her photograph. Try to send me her photograph so that you can start the process." I asked him to send me a bill of what it would cost. The amount was a revelation to me. The bill contained boxes of candles, transportation fares, food, accommodation, and many others. Nine hundred and ninety-seven thousand naira in all to start with!

"That's about one million naira," I said over the phone.

"Yes. You will be satisfied with what they do," he assured me.

I was silent for a while ruminating on how many Nigerians could start this type of treatment with one million naira.

He broke the silence.

"Pay it and get your daughter on her feet," he said, as if ordering me.

"It is not the amount of money," I said. "Of course, I could afford it. But how many people can afford this if this is a therapy from the Catholic Church? Is there any assurance?" I asked.

"Don't doubt them. They have been protecting me all these years. If it were not for them, I would have been dead. My children would have been dead too!"

They must be very good, I thought. I was still digesting the spiritual power of this priestly band of prayer warriors and intercessors and wondering why they are so secret and only known to a select group of rich Nigerians. My friend explained more about these priests who perform miracles.

"These are very spiritual people, more powerful than witches, more powerful than *adjenes*, self-confessing wizards. They investigate your background at night and nip in the bud whatever attack is being planned against you. They can even go to your Okpara village without being seen or known and find out about those planning mischief against you," he concluded.

I was amazed at their power. Priests who said Mass during the day and in the depth of night flying to places to investigate spiritual plans to attack someone and his or her family.

"How long will this treatment take?" I asked.

"It could take three, six, nine months or even a year or longer. When they need to pray, they will be brought together and you provide the candles and what they need to go on with their praying mission."

"It means they may have more than one session?" I asked.

"It depends on the gravity of the case," he told me.

"OK, let me think about it and come back to you," I told him.

"Make up your mind fast," he told me.

"You know I am trying a masseur who appears now to be doing a good job," I told him.

"Leave the masseur, leave going to T.B. Joshua as some folks are bound to advise you. If your daughter gets up on her legs through T.B. Joshua, three months later we will be attending your funeral," he told me.

"How do you know that?" I asked.

"It is an attack and those ones don't know how to deal with spiritual attacks. T.B. Joshua would take the spirit of the attack from her and give it back to you," he explained.

I did not know much about T.B, Joshua but I felt my friend could not be the spokesman for him. I was not in a mood to argue about who was better at casting out demons, the secret society of reverend fathers or T.B. Joshua.

My friend looked good. He was careful about what he ate and drank and was very meticulous about everything. He did not eat eggs, no bread, no dairy product, and no beef. He occasionally ate fish. He ate *moin moin* and *akara*, bean foods, as also *ikuoka*, a boiled corn meal. He is prosperous and has achieved a lot in his profession and is sought after for workshops and other contract jobs in addition to his job as a professor. He is a damned hard worker, Americans would say of him. He wakes by five and goes to bed just before midnight. He has excellent education and he is bright. He is very focused in his profession and I am not surprised that he is so successful. But he attributes his wellbeing to other factors. The Catholic priests must be taking good care of him.

After resting for two days, we started to go out. I mean my wife, Eloho, and I. We had lived in Maidguri for about a decade as I taught at the University of Maiduguri. While there, Barrister had been my best friend and promoter. Older than me with over ten years, he was a very successful lawyer and everybody knew him. He did very well. He had plenty of property in town as in Bauchi, Warri, and even in London. Once in a while he took me to the buffet at Lake Chad Hotel where the rich enjoyed themselves. I couldn't on my own go to the buffet but he invited me several times. I also got to the Chinese Restaurant, which was very exclusive, once or twice with him. He was back in Sapele after retiring from active work and getting tired of living far away from home. He had a small office at Sapele, a small room with his name plate on the door; he was no longer a practicing attorney in the real sense of the word. He only signed agreements on land deals and simple agreements that needed a lawyer as a witness.

We decided to go and visit him. Most times I came home alone and I took it as a duty to visit him. This time I wanted to go with Anne and Eloho to see him and his Gwoza wife who had retired from the civil service in Maiduguri and was now with him in Sapele. By now, her native Gwoza and even Maiduguri in Borno have been devastated by the scourge of Boko Haram. So, to Sapele we went.

One of my discoveries in this one year in Nigeria is that almost everybody has become very religious and people often showed it in the programs they watch on television. I guess I am not religious because I like to watch news. But when you arrive at a host's house and the first statement upon entering is, "I hope you watch T.B. Joshua's Emmanuel Television," I immediately realized we were in for a proselytizing session. "He is very good. He is the only pastor that really does miracles. All the others are fake ones," Barrister said.

I had heard of the man and the miracles he performed but did not know him or other churches well to pass any judgment.

"Do you watch Emmanuel TV?"

"No, I don't think it is on my DSTV," I answered.

"Oh, it is on the Street Cable. It is only five hundred naira and you are connected," he pronounced.

I did not know there was something called Street Cable that was illegally connected to one's television to view at an insignificant fraction of the cost of DSTV.

Barrister and his wife were so absorbed by Emmanuel TV as if we were disrupting an intense experience.

"Satan must be crushed!" Barrister shouted.

"Amen," his wife answered.

They soon realized that they had visitors. I looked so bemused that they must have realized that they were performing a comical act before their guests. It was only after then that they asked us to sit down. Ten minutes or more of standing to watch our hosts enraptured in an Emmanuel Television program!

"You need to take your daughter to the Synagogue in Lagos. T.B. Joshua will heal her. She will come back on her legs. My wife can follow your wife and Eloho and go and see T.B. Joshua," he advised.

"They have a hotel for those who come from overseas. Many people come from America, England, South Africa, and Korea to seek cures for their ailments. I am one hundred percent sure that once you take her there, she will walk back. There will be no need for a wheelchair. Do you see the miracles he performs daily? You must try it before they go back to the United States and you will marvel at the spiritual power of T.B. Joshua."

"Have you been to the Synagogue?" I asked.

"Yes. I went there for my eyes. I can barely see now. They say I have glaucoma. Even as I talk now I can't see you properly," he explained.

"He is blind. He can't see at all. He only pretends seeing what he can't see," his wife cut in.

"Don't mind her. Yes, I went to the Synagogue for my eyes. I know why I could not be cured," he confessed. I asked the why question.

"I did not have the faith," he said humbly.

I had a lot to think about. Do the mad people and others who seek cures and are said to be healed, do they have faith before they are cured?

But what intrigues me the most is a man who could not be cured at the Synagogue recommending the same place to me and a hundred percent sure that my daughter would be healed. My daughter would have the faith he did not have, he must believe.

Before we went back to Effurun, Anne and I offered to bring him to the United States for surgery to remedy his eyes' problems. He would get a visa and stay with us for the surgery of the two eyes that his faith did not allow T.B. Joshua to heal with a miracle but which Dr. Herbert Greenman would do with laser surgery in Charlotte, North Carolina.

None of my two friends recommending spiritual treatment for my daughter knew we had tried Elele where a charismatic priest did his best in prayers. My wife took Eloho there for five days literally sleeping on a mat outside and praying with the priest. None of my two friends knew Anne had virtually stayed with Eloho for treatment for six weeks at Ughelli. There the herbalist might have seen treating the daughter of someone in America as a source of income and sustenance. He was slow in administering what he even knew and wanted Anne and Eloho to stay six months, which Anne couldn't do because of her job. She was lucky not to be fired from her hospital work after unilaterally extending her leave by two more weeks. None of my friends advising on where to take my daughter for treatment knew that Evangelist Emmanuel was treating her more as a masseur with herbs in this visit. Her limbs were getting relaxed and she could do better with a walker. Eloho noticed some improvement. But soon Evangelist Emmanuel who was not a pastor was asking for money to buy candles and perfumes to pray and treat her. Even before Anne and Eloho would leave, he lost his mother-in-law and wanted a hefty loan together with the handsome fee I paid him.

I made inquiries about both the Catholic group of intercessors and T.B. Joshua. Father Abaka is my wife's family friend. In fact, they both grew up in Warri and their mothers were close friends. So close are they that over twenty-five years after our traditional wedding, Father Abaka consecrated our marriage at St. Jude's Church in Effurun. It was a very low-key ceremony with only two couples invited: the Onojegbes and the Akpotus. So he was somebody we were very close to. Besides, he is a very experienced reverend father who has gone to Rome and he is a Superior Father. I have always felt that much as I mistrust reverend fathers and pastors generally, he is one of the very few I trust. You could see in him one with a missionary passion and the Catholic Church often sent him to start new parishes and transferred him to new places once he has established one. His plan at Ebrumede Catholic Church shows a devoted priest who cares for the souls and lives of the people. Had he been in a different continent, he could have risen to a Bishop or more with his good work. But the Warri or Delta bishopric was one in which ethnicity and other "bad belle" politics did not reward good work. It was the bishopric that brought an assistant white priest to be bishop because of the clashes among the Urhobo, Igbo, Itsekiri, and Isoko, among so many groups. That clergy would later resign after being transferred to Benin and made a bishop. He did it with shame after a scandalous affair with a teenage girl. Warri's internal church strife would not allow good ones to thrive, a Catholic woman told me.

I had to ask Father Abaka about the Catholic group being recommended to me.

"Father, have you heard of a Catholic group that heals folks like my daughter in a wheelchair?" I asked.

"There are Charismatic priests who do that. In fact, there is one at Orerokpe and I can either connect you to him or send your daughter's name to him for prayers," he told me.

"No, Father, this group is not the Charismatic one. They are brought together from different parishes across the country and one buys candles for them to pray. One pays for their transportation to the place, pay for their hotel accommodation or wherever they choose to stay, and pay for the food they eat to break their fasts," I explained to him.

"Prof, I don't know of any such group in the Catholic Church," he assured me. "If there is, I believe I would have known."

"What do you advise I do in connection with taking my daughter there?"

"There is no such group that I know of. And for all the money for those things, I don't think it is a Catholic group."

"I am told they need one million naira to start the program that could last three, six months or even more than a year," I further explained.

"I believe we should try the Orerokpe Reverend Father."

My conversation reinforced our decision to try hospitals and masseurs and prayers rather than the Catholic group. I had to call two people, a friend's sister and my late friend's wife in Lagos, to ask about T.B. Joshua. They acknowledged hearing about his performing miracles. Both are strong members of their respective churches: one a strong Catholic and the other a member of the Mountain of Fire and Miracles. I knew they could be biased when asked about another church doing miracles while theirs do not. I was going to depend on commonsense rather than what I expected would not be objective.

"I don't trust his miracles are Christian. You never can tell where some pastors get their powers nowadays. Don't worsen the situation because I heard he takes away from somewhere and gives back in another way," Queen explained. I understood the cryptic language.

"Nobody knows exactly where he derives his power from," she said.

My friend's sister rejection was more categorical.

"Don't go there. Don't cause your family more problems!" she pronounced.

She must have discussed my daughter's case with her brother. I remember the scary warning against going to the Synagogue.

After Anne and Eloho flew back to Charlotte, I heard that my Lagos friend's daughter was involved in a ghastly accident which broke her spinal cord. I telephoned him to offer my sympathies.

"Yes, it's no joke. I can feel now what you feel with a disabled child," he told me.

"It is not easy," I told him.

"I am preparing to fly her to London for surgery. I don't think any hospital in Nigeria can do her any good and time is of the essence."

Three days later his daughter was flown to London and left the airport straight in an ambulance to the hospital where successful surgery was performed on her.

"Congratulations for the successful surgery," I wrote my friend who had accompanied his daughter to London. Two weeks after his return from London, he told me that his daughter would stay in the hospital for another month before rehabilitation would begin.

"Have you and your wife made up your minds on your daughter's treatment?"
I had not answered before he went on.

"My daughter's case was a car accident. Yours was an 'attack' that needs spiritual solution. Why worry about one million naira when you can help others with more than that amount?" he asked.

I knew he asked that question because he was privy to some help I had given to another friend. I had been ready to contribute as much as four million naira to assist resolve a problem that befell a friend. Now he meant I was not serious about my own daughter because I was not ready to part with only one million naira to start a process of healing prayers. I thought it was too much to question my love of my daughter and doing it in the amount of money I was ready to spend on the secret healing priests he was recommending.

"Discuss with your wife and start the prayer-healing process as soon as possible. As I have told you, she will walk maybe in three months, six months, nine months, or a year and more but those priests have the spiritual power to heal her," he told me.

"I will get back to you on this," I said.

"Let me warn you again. Don't go to any other place, T.B. Joshua, Mercyland, or any Evangelist. If you do that and your daughter begins to walk on her own, three months later we will be at your funeral."

He had added Mercyland to the list of places that I should not go to. Mercyland was a new ministry in Jakpa Road, Effurun. In recent months it had become popular with sick and troubled Nigerians seeking miracles from the church's senior pastor.

I did not understand who was the "we" attending my funeral. But did I need to ask him questions when he says that only his secret group was the only means for my daughter's safe healing?

By this time, Barrister had flown to Charlotte for his eye surgery. I was still in Nigeria. He was not just legally blind but really blind. It was Efe, my neighbor's son, who was going to school in Charlotte that practically led him. He was put in a wheelchair to his seat in the plane and would be on a wheelchair outside the plane for his comfort. He would phone me from Charlotte as I was still in Effurun that it was a good decision that I asked Efe to guide him. By the time he went for surgery, I had already arrived in Charlotte.

Barrister opened up after the first eye surgery. He told me about the painless and efficient laser surgery he went through. He also told me so many people with eye problems had botched surgeries in Nigeria and were now blind.

"Nigeria is still very backward," he said. He continued: "Could you imagine that a consultant at the University Teaching Hospital told me that I would never see again?"

He couldn't tell his wife who was waiting for him outside. But ironically, the wife knew all along that he couldn't see.

I could not fathom some things in Nigeria. Is this a case of misery loving company? Or already trapped, they want more to be trapped in their company. But I think of faith and irrationality. My daughter has spastic paralysis and American doctors have been doing their best to make life more convenient and comfortable for her. I waited for my Lagos friend to call and ask me again about the spiritual treatment. He had told me that the priests who protected him and his family were scattered by the jealous Catholic hierarchy, hence the daughter was involved in an accident. According to him, if they had been in their proper places, nothing would have affected his daughter. My wife and I have chosen the medical line for what has been diagnosed as a medical problem.

7

BREATHING SPACES: VISITING OTHER COUNTRIES

During the more than one year I was in Nigeria, I traveled outside the country three times. I took trips to Colombia for the Medellin International Poetry Festival in July 2013; to New Delhi, India, for the Sahitya Akademi World Poetry Festival in March 2014; and to Johannesburg, South Africa, for the African Literature Association annual conference in April 2014. I came back from each of these trips with albums and memories of historic and cultural places and figures and I wonder what my country has to offer others as those countries have offered me. A country in which history is not studied is bound to suffer irreparably and perhaps irreversibly from its past mistakes. I know that at The University of North Carolina at Charlotte, and I believe in many American universities and colleges, the history department is one of the largest, perhaps next to English in the large College of Liberal Arts and Sciences. History is a very important component of the humanities. A people who grow up not knowing their history cannot be as united as those who do. A people who do not learn from the mistakes of their history are a lost group. A people who are not proud of historical achievements have nothing to celebrate. A people who do not study their history may find it difficult to imbibe the sense of patriotism. The federal and state governments should rethink their attitude towards history in the curriculum at the various levels of elementary, secondary, and tertiary education.

In Medellin, Colombia, there are memorial statues of heroes in history, politics, and the arts. There are sculptures of historical figures in public spaces and museums showcasing the works of their artists to tourists and locals. Bolivar who liberated half the South American continent is omnipresent in museums and parks. He stands tall in marble and bronze in parks all over Medellin and I believe in other Central Andean towns. What later came to be known as Bolivarian revolution is in that marble sculpture and it spread across the Central Andean nations to result in the independence of Bolivia, Colombia, Peru, and Venezuela. Of the artists, poets are celebrated with their statues in public parks. Botero, the painter most identified with Colombia, has sections of museums totally dedicated to his work.

Colombia impressed me with its interest in history, culture, arts, and recreational activities. Surely, it is not a rich country as such but it appears there is state effort to foist the people's history in public places to be seen by everybody. That is what I see in the statues in the parks and the museums. Many of us poets were taken to different parts of Colombia. I was taken to a small mountain town where there was a town center, an imposing Catholic church that was built for over forty years, and much to know about the folk life of Central Andeans. Even in such a small town, the streets were cobbled with stones and there was excellent drainage. There were small parks and we read from our poetry to a sizable audience in one of them. I believe these people know how to relax from what I observed.

Here's a poem my Colombian experience inspired:

Medellin Testament
1. Of Bolivar* and Liberation

It's not surprising that in marble Bolivar stands
tall in the market-center beside the cathedral.
Along the street pastry shops whose aroma
tempts me to break the fast that's not yet due.
But in the market, steps of the cathedral,
and adjoining streets a sprawling destitute army

sitting disheveled or lying down as if lifeless.
For what was the liberation to these beggars?

In the nearby park, baseball capped seniors
in T-shirts exercising and walking past misery.
Facing the park again another gothic church
and in marble heroes, poets, and the Virgin Mary;
a past in which every heart beat with contentment.
In the early Saturday morning young ones out—
life flows all forms of detritus and disruptions.
Here in Medellin I have not heard of Escobar,
nor the rusty guns of FARC in the forest.

2. At the Museo Antioquia

At the Antioquia Museum, Botero's voluminous
women and figures that define him Colombian.
Some other artist paints *Bandit Woman* black
to perjure the voiceless and still get paid for it.
Another paints a sweet black child, fruits on her lap,
as if to fend off hunger that's poaching her kinsfolks.

Bolivar stands tall after liberating half a continent
with men trained in Haiti for the revolution.
The Haitian host, asked for recompense, simply said:
"Don't mention my name!" Of course, Bolivar felt
such goodness should not be buried in the chest.
For history to tell the truth, he proclaimed the name!

- Bolivar (1783—1830): liberator of Colombia, Venezuela, Ecuador, and Peru.

In New Delhi, it is as if India was not colonized by the same
imperial Britain that colonized Nigeria. But what a difference

on monuments, historical, and cultural sites! The Gandhi memorial is like a shrine and receives millions of Indian and foreign visitors yearly. I went to pay my respects to the great world leader of peaceful protests and great martyr for the poor of India. There are guides, historians, who tell you about each monument. I was at the Red Fort, headquarters of the Moguls who once ruled India, then of the British whose imprints are still clearly preserved. The Gate near the hotel I stayed is one of such tourist destinations. The Muslim forts and palaces, the Bahia White Tulip Temple, and four hours away by road or train the Taj Mahal are strong tourist attractions. New Delhi is spaciously planned and there are parks here and there for relaxation.

Delhi is highly populated and has about the same intense energy as Lagos but it appears orderly in many ways. Drivers appear to be more civil. The maruti, the Nigerian keke-na-pep, drives mindful of traffic laws. It is impressive that the Sahitya Akademi organizes a world poetry festival into which it pours so much money to bring poets from over thirty countries across continents. I was one of the two African poets there. My other African is a lady from The Seychelles.

I think of Nigeria and I envisage lepers lining the Ore-Benin Road, the potholed roads all over the country, the armed robbers, kidnapers, brainless drivers on the roads, and the careless culture of the people and the Government towards their past. At the Benin Museum in Ring Road, near the Oba's Palace, so many empty glass cages of missing artefacts. We might be struggling to bring back to Nigeria the Benin and other Nigerian artworks looted or stolen from us by Europeans but we have not been able to keep and maintain what we have. The same story is true of the National Museum in Lagos. What is the Ministry of Culture and Tourism doing? Nigeria is not a tourist destination to anybody outside! We should ask ourselves why.

I have this poetic reflection of India and Nigeria while in New Delhi:

India

To celebrate Tagore's laurels with songs, I come here
where my people seek remedies for serious afflictions.

I hear my folks seeking invincibility also come here
for massive reinforcements against spiritual attacks;

they would travel here and wherever provides
resources to overcome perils littering their homes!

India, the great mirror they hold up, a wand
and who gets there would learn all the magic

and return with the singular insight of body
and spirit in their parallel worlds of residence.

India of my youth conjures up charms of love
but my Ayesiri's already refuged in my bosom

and the minstrel needs no charms he who composes
and sings songs and dances to enrapture his beauty!

Once at the Delhi Airport a palmist read my palms
but I would not pay a fee for the unsolicited service

I who come from the land of Ominigbo, martyred one
seeing through the future with eyes of a scouting god!

I bow at shrines of my hosts' gods, marvelous figures;
I offer bananas, flowers, and coins at the temple of Shriva.

It's hard to tell which land holds more mysteries—
both, for sure, lands of spirits with parallel lives.

Do Indians see my land and people with equal awe
and solidarity of the same world as we do theirs?

We reside at opposite ends of the ocean they claim
but contend with the same spirits of different tongues

that life unleashes at us from every possible direction,
and I pronounce my land and India universe of spirits

where the shadow and the body live separate lives
that tug each other so fiercely in parallel worlds.

And so we share afflictions of poverty and disease
but open the door to necessary health and wellbeing.

I come to familiar land in New Delhi despite alien rites
and so my kinsfolks and I are very much at home here.

        I had been to Durban before this trip to Johannesburg
from April 6 to 16, 2014. We, Nigerians, always console
ourselves by saying that our circumstances are different from
those of others and would say that after all Caucasians ruled
South Africa till recently; hence so many things appear to
work smoothly in South Africa. I don't accept that excuse for
our inability to learn from history or make history a guiding
beacon for our future. Earlier in October 2006, while in
Durban, I was in a group bused to talk about poetry to high
school students. After the talk, we visited the nearby town of
KwaDukuza (formerly Stanger) to see Shaka's tomb. It is still
well maintained up till now. I believe many South Africans
and outsiders come there for inspiration of a great African
leader despite his flaws. He founded the Zulu nation. It is the

largest ethnic group in South Africa but small compared to bigger Nigerian groups but its sense of nationalism and maintenance of their culture is uniquely strong. I am not surprised that Jacob Zuma, their president, dances effortlessly to Zulu music and polyrhythms.

Everywhere in Johannesburg is replete with images of the country's history—pre-apartheid, apartheid, anti-apartheid struggle, and post-apartheid of the new South Africa. Protea Hotel, where I stayed while in Johannesburg, stood across the road from CODESA (COSATU?), the trade union headquarters of Black workers. Cyril Ramaphosa used to be the Secretary-General until a few years into Mandela's presidency when he resigned to go into business. From the Protea Hotel, I walked through the Mandela Bridge. I saw what was described to me as apartheid architecture— rectangular, almost box-like, tall buildings to show apartheid's power! In the tourist buses, from the earphones one listened to the history of Johannesburg from its beginning as Egoli, the City of Gold, to the present. I walked up Constitution Hill. I took a tour bus to Soweto and learnt passionately at close quarters the history of apartheid. The Soweto Massacre is memorialized in parks and sculptures. There is history everywhere engraved in stone and marble. Perhaps the most moving is seeing Mandela's House and beside it, in Vilikazi Street, Desmond Tutu's house. Further away and covered by orchards stood Winnie Mandela's house. The female guide showed us the new and big hotel in Soweto where Barack Obama stayed when in Soweto as well as numerous installations and sculptures expressing the Soweto experience. I saw the squatter structures without light and water. Apartheid has gone but the vestiges of its consequence still abound. South Africans are not ashamed of their past despite the shame, violence, and pain in it. Rather, they remind themselves of that hurtful era as they want their future to be far better than the past. It appears that Nigerians want to forget their past.

I was in Johannesburg when the trial of Oscar Pistorius was going on. Many people were glued to the television to watch whether the athlete deliberately or accidentally killed his girlfriend. I saw the excitement in the air as two soccer teams in the South African Football League, the Bafana Bafana Boys and one other major team, were about to play a match. I left Johannesburg with a strong desire to return to see and know more about South Africa and its history. I am yet to go to Robben Island. I am yet to see many of the parks. I have an unfinished business in South Africa.

Whom have we memorialized in Nigerian history? Where do we see anything to remind one of Dr. Aggrey and Herbert Macaulay, our great nationalists? What of our first-generation political leaders such as Sir Ahmadu Bello, Sir Tafawa Balewa, Dr. Nnamdi Azikiwe, and Chief Obafemi Awolowo? To me two of the great Nigerian heroes in recent history are Colonel Fajuyi, who gave up his life rather than surrender his guest General Aguiyi Ironsi to killers, and General Murtala Muhammed. What have we done to make the current generation and future generations remember them for what they have done for the country. What of General Idiagbon whose joint leadership with General Buhari many of us feel should have been the beginning of a disciplined society if their rule was not aborted by Ibrahim Babangida's coup? We fought a civil war for over two years in which millions of mainly Igbo people lost their lives either killed in the battlefield or died from starvation. What have we done to commemorate the unity of the nation? Where are memorials for the innocent Igbos who died from the massacres and the civil war itself? At Umuahia there is the Ojukwu Bunker, which I visited in the mid-1980s. What has happened to it? Much could be done to mark Opi where Christopher Okigbo, one of Africa's greatest poets, died. There is so much to do that is not yet done to keep our history alive and as a source of inspiration to future generations.

One feels disgusted with the long list of those being offered the Order of the Niger yearly. I am not disgusted by everybody because there are a few good ones in the long list. But national honors have become banal; a mockery of a nation's sense of dignity. National honors are lobbied for or given for political affiliations, and very many with questionable characters ironically receive what are supposed to be sacred. With the massive desecration, these awards might as well be given to vultures, dogs, and donkeys with political affiliations. In fact, most of the appointees to the National Conference need not be there.

Let it not be known that I am not giving up on this issue. I see that in some parts of the country, there already exist cultural and national icons that could be promoted. The Ooni of Ife's palace is a good example and while history may not officially be taught now there is a feeling that the Yoruba as a group have a good sense of their history and culture, especially in the folklore of Oduduwa and the deities. Badagry is known for preserving some of the relics of slave trade days. There are other institutions that deserve praise. I was struck by the Lamido of Adamawa's palace in Yola with an impressive museum attached to the palace with reminiscences of the coming of Europeans to the area and the founding of the emirate. Sir Ahmadu Bello's tomb is well preserved in Sokoto and visitors see it. I am very impressed by Aminu Kano's simple tomb preserved in a compound that now hosts a modern conference center in Kano. The place is well maintained and there are guides taking visitors round and explaining the mallam's radical political ideology which has distinguished Kano from other northern states up to this day. In Nembe and Brass in Bayelsa State, I also saw what could be more exposed to fellow Nigerians and outsiders—monuments and testimonies to the Lander Brothers' exploration and different dynasties of kings with their mausoleums still well maintained. Brass still shows off the racial cemetery and some of the earliest outposts of Europeans in Nigeria.

Appealing to the Nigerian Government over issues of history and culture that drive tourism is like talking to somebody dumb and deaf. How do you expect a Government whose institutions deal with, for instance, aviation, railway, and telephone that have collapsed or died, to do anything? Why should there be a ministry of tourism that does not have statistics of tourists visiting the country and to what parts? A country without accountability for money voted for ministries or parastatals is not just stupid but bankrupt-minded. It is my hope as I see nothing about our history and culture studied and promoted in the curriculum and in the media that a fresh rethinking will take place. History matters, if we want a country of patriotic citizens. History matters if we want to avoid the mistakes of the past and move boldly forward for the good of the generality of citizens. History binds people together. Individuals, institutions, and the state should do more to memorialize our historical and cultural figures. Much as we have become individualized, there is still much sense in the collective spirit of a people that the Kenyan philosopher, John Mbiti, has succinctly described as "I am because we are!"

8

NATIONAL RECREATIONS

I saw Nigerians taking to sports, relaxation, and entertainment as never before. I saw this as a welcome trend. But we still have so much to catch up with since real vacations are rare. It is not common for the few vacationing to go to places where they will not go on a buying spree of clothes and even articles to sell. How many Nigerians does one see in holiday spots across the world? How is Tinapa Resort faring? What of Ikogosi Warm and Cold Springs Resort? How many go to Obudu Ranch? Is the Yankari Game Reserve still functioning? It is easy to slip into comparing Nigerians to other nationals on many aspects. That is not a bad thing really because we occupy the same universe and in a global era Nigerians and other nationals interface inextricably.

I have called the observations here national recreations to loosely put together my personal experiences on the recreational attitudes of Nigerians—concepts of vacations, parks, museums, sports, relaxation, entertainment, and other things of the sort. How many Nigerians take two weeks off their normal routines to have a vacation? How many choose Nigerian destinations? During the summer and the Christmas seasons many Nigerians go abroad on "vacation." Some of them go and stay with relatives in European or North American cities. Others go to Dubai to stay in hotels or their own condos they keep for only those seasons of the year. But where do they go in those places as vacationers?

There are not many parks or national monuments in Nigeria to visit. The United States, for instance, has the National Parks Commission that takes care of parks and tourist resorts such as the Yellowstone National Park and other famous American resorts. The Yellowstone and the Yosemite Parks in Colorado and California respectively blow your mind away with an appreciation of nature's wonders. In 1964 the American Government passed the Wilderness Act to set aside some lands to remain untouched by logging and development. How much of nature do we see and appreciate in Nigeria? That we live in the tropical rainforest and grasslands is not enough that we enjoy nature. There are views that we need to develop to produce optic sensation in an aesthetic sense. The Ikogosi Warm and Cold Springs Resort has attempted that in an amazing way and it gladdens my heart that one is exposed to nature in an eco-friendly manner. I will say more on this beautiful resort of warm and cold springs later.

We who lived in the forest before modernization opened up places ought to incorporate nature into our living experiences but we seem not to care about trees, rivers, lakes, hills, and other aspects of nature. From my observation in this period and earlier, we tend to be destructive of nature rather than nurturing or nursing it. We set forests and grasslands afire and destroy the natural ecology. We do not preserve our wildlife, the fauna and flora that are part of the cycle that binds human and non-human lives. We hunt without replenishing the wilds. We fish without replenishing the waters. I notice that we catch shoals of baby fish and relish them. What will someday mature into big fish? We have not learnt to throw back the small fish we catch for them to grow and reproduce so that there is always more fish in the waters. We cut down forest trees and poach our forests to death and we are left with open landscapes. In the name of making farms to grow crops we burn our forests and grasslands. During the dry season, and especially the harmattan period, many wild fires break out without concerted effort to put them out or contain them. Such fires virtually devour the forest or grassland and the eco-diverse population. There was a time when forests formed a green canopy overhead. The forests provided leaves, herbs, roots, and barks for medicines, traditional and modern. So, in destroying the forests, we are limiting our medicinal options for cures. Researchers still go to the Amazons in South America to study what medicinal cures the forest can provide. In our patch of the earth, we have beheaded our trees and decimated much of the non-human lives among us. Many people so relish the so-called "bush meat" that wild animals are hunted to fill the appetites of such people.

By breaking the wonderful bond between human and non-human lives we are destroying the cycle of life. Trees are cut down in villages, towns, and cities on the superstitious ground that witches use them to convene in their covens. Long ago we had forest reserves but today they are shadows of themselves. Agricultural officers used to have camps and stayed in the forest for training to study the species of trees. One wonders what obtains today. Students and their teachers would probably live in the city and drive there and forge information and return as having completed the internship they never did in the forest. The forests are important as providers of food for sustenance and herbs and barks for medicinal purposes. We need more food and sources of cures for old and new ailments and we just have to revive our dying forests.

The United States has museums ranging from the Getty to the Smithsonian where art works are displayed. Wealthy individuals founded them or left endowments for the founding of these museums for which they are remembered. They left a legacy of greatness in giving out. So today one can go to the Smithsonian National Museum of African Art and see for free works of African art being exhibited. On the other hand, Nigerians still seem to be trapped by the culture of material acquisition but die forgotten. As I recapitulate this, the United States is planning releasing to the Nigerian Government over three billion dollars that Sani Abacha stashed in the United States alone. One can imagine what he stashed in Europe, especially Switzerland and Britain. You can imagine what that money could have been used for if not stolen. Or, already stolen, what contributions he would have made to the country's arts and culture if he had founded an endowment with the staggering sum of money. We have had so many wealthy individuals but, after their deaths, who still remembers them? I think of Odutola of the tire fame and other rich entrepreneurs. The Ibru Organization, headed by Michael Ibru, has collapsed without a monument. Maybe Theophilus Danjuma is doing something with the so much money he has but time will tell if he is remembered through a major endowment he initiates.

These museums in the United States, as in Europe, sharpen the aesthetic taste of a people. Visit the Mint Museum in Charlotte, North Carolina; the Metropolitan in New York; the British Museum, the Tate, and Madame Tussauds Wax Museum in London; Musee de l'Homme in Paris, and the many art museums in Madrid, Rome, and Amsterdam. I have earlier spoken of Medellin, Colombia, with Botero's collections. Look at Mount Rushmore with iconic faces of American Presidents! Visit Washington, DC, and see how historical figures and national heroes are memorialized. London bristles with monuments of English heroic figures. There are monuments everywhere showing visitors, young and old, about their nation's great figures. For the nationals, it should be an inspiring experience to live among so many heroes. My friend, Joe Obi, a sociologist, describes the phenomenon of memorializing as "civil religion," the idea of consecrating one's national heroes whether in India, Colombia, or South Africa. If Nigerians are to have true vacations at home or bring in tourists, they need to develop parks, not just empty playing fields called parks and museums. As human beings, we need to be close to nature and our past heroes. What will anybody come to Nigeria for if there is nothing to click and keep in a camera or a smart phone? Tourists will use a selfie to capture their being with a hero, historical and so memorialized, or an iconic place.

But there is much to commend too in national trends in Nigeria. Despite the often tense atmosphere in Jos, I saw so many walking in the morning and at other times. I spent the Christmas/New Year holiday period with my friend and his family in Jos. The Tin City has no doubt lost its luster in many ways. It is no longer the holiday destination of expatriates in Nigeria as it used to be till the late 1970s. The great zoo is overgrown with weeds. The lone lion kept there died from starvation. No doubt the keepers who were poor stole the funds or food meant to feed the lion for the survival of their families! The great museum nearby that used to boast of the best collection of ceramics in sub-Saharan Africa has been looted empty! The nearby dam is no longer a dam from neglect. The roads do not show a city that has been there benefitting from industry and government projects. NABISCO, Rock Beer, and spring water are still there but only NABISCO still stands on its feet. The tin mines that brought nationalities from the northeast, the middle belt, and the south have now become mere burrow pits. The wealth the mines engendered squandered away. As for the NOK terra cottas that make museums and galleries proud in New York and Europe, nothing remains!

I had been in Jos when there was the Christmas bombing and the Hausa-Birom conflict, configured into a Christian-Muslim conflict, took place during the latter part of December of 2011. There were killings by Muslims and Christians, but that was an earlier period. Others I told I was going to Jos for my 2013 Christmas felt I was seeking martyrdom in a city I have been emotionally attached to since the early 80s. But that was not just the case. Ola is a great friend and I love spending as much time as possible with him and his family. And so I stayed with him in his barricaded house on the Old Legislative Quarters' Road in the broadly called Angwa Rukuba area of Jos. Whenever outside and I looked to the front of the house the rocky mountain takes my breath away. As a walker, I soon took to walking in the morning. I did the first two days alone before Ola decided to be accompanying me. We walked through the Old Bukuru Road past some waterworks and dams on a road that must have been tarred in colonial or First Republic times. The tar has now peeled away. It is a mountainous trail with rocks of different shapes rising to the sky. Some of the rocks appear to have fallen on others while many rock formations seem to be moving at the rate of just a few yards in a millennium. Rocks are never in a hurry to move, if at all they move. On this trail we pass so many young, middle-aged, and old people walking up and down the rocky and mountainous trail. We cross bridges over streams murmuring their way to unknown destinations but perhaps not too far away. We pass what Ola describes as an Irish Bridge of water flowing over concrete slabs. We ascend the winding road on a rocky hill to the top where there is a dam that has lost much of its draughts. We sit on some rocks overlooking a large expanse of beautiful naturally endowed landscape. Some herdsmen herd cows on the rocky terrain. We do about three to four miles one way and stop not too far from the new Jos University Teaching Hospital (JUTH) at the end of that winding road. That was the colonial road that ran straight to Bukuru from Angwa Rukuba which now has a far longer road over a terrain without rocky hills. We turn back after a few minutes of rest, sitting and admiring the craft of nature with the rock formations. Jos has the culture of walking and exercising and I learn it started from colonial times with so many expatriates walking and exercising.

I like the Jabi Lake area of Abuja. It was thoughtful of the original city planners to designate a large expanse of land around the lake for recreation. There, in the morning, people come from different parts of the city to walk, jog, or do other exercises, and even play Ping Pong. A few horses were there for riding for a fee. Most of the horses did not seem well taken care of because they looked dirty and lean. I went there many times in the cool air of early morning to walk round three to four times before sunup. A few times I played table tennis with some young guys that came there to play and make two hundred naira from each interested player. The lake is generally well kept and neat. The view here is awesome as the sun rises in an orange glow in the east and showering rainbow colors over the water. I almost rented a studio room from across the street but being asked to pay for two years when I was supposed to be there for a maximum of five months made me lose it. The last I heard of Jabi Lake is that the recreation ground is being sold to a private person who would use it for parties or maybe sell it for more housing in the fast growing city.

The rest of Abuja has some parks and gyms. I knew of Rockview Hotel and its gym. I did some treadmill work there. It has lawn tennis and much as I would have liked to play, I had no partner. I understand there are many gyms in Abuja and one registers for the year to enjoy the facilities.

Wafi man no dey carry last! That is the saying by Warri folks. By fair or foul means, Warri folks do not come last. I was pleasantly surprised that the Petroleum Training Institute Staff Club housed a gym. I walked in the morning on weekdays within the PTI facilities and went to the gym after registering in the Club that was open to outsiders. My having taught at PTI from 1975 to 1977 as a pioneer teaching staff did not make me a free member! It is a fairly small gym like most of the Nigerian gyms I have seen. In one room are the treadmill, cycling machines, and one or two other machines. Another room is used by a trainer (also called coach) for thrice weekly exercises—Monday and Wednesday from five to six o'clock in the evening and on Saturday from eight to nine in the morning. At its fullest it had some twelve folks and the trainer at a time but attendance was up and down.

There is a hall where parties are held by those who reserve it for weekends. It is in that spacious place that ping pong is played. At times two boards are assembled there but for the most part only one board is used. I had a table tennis buddy in Jude, a staff in the institution's business office. I went for the gym exercise with the coach when Jude was not around. However, I had a passion for ping pong which I had been playing since my secondary school days in Obinomba in the 1960s. The nostalgia that brought me to table tennis also brought others who saw us playing and joined us. We had a young man come in once in a while. He was interested in winning games but we were interested in exercising ourselves and having fun. The irony of it was that the more serious Daniel was, the more he lost. For me, in the days of insecurity in the Delta, going to play table tennis with Jude superseded other activities at that time and I had a good time with a jolly fellow.

Once in a while I overheard gossips in the gym or drinking place in the Club. Once when the coach did not show up but sent his assistant, a young lady who had dropped out for not paying her fees saw me in town.

"I hear the gym don fall. I hear say the coach don gain weight," she said.

"When last were you at the gym?" I asked.

"E don tay," she answered.

"How you know say the place don fall?" I asked.

"Na so I hear-o," she said.

It was the typical way of rumor-mongering in Warri. I could only laugh. I told her the coach was around the previous day and he was as fit as ever. At the drinking place large television screens on the walls were always tuned to football. It was there a young Nigerian was boasting to everybody that he could die for Arsenal.

The English Premier League and European Football are engines of globalization feeding on a captive Nigerian audience. But they have not always been so. Yes, in the 1960s and 1970s I heard of English and Australian football clubs through Pools. As a young man, I was told that whoever played Pools would hardly make it in life because it was addictive and nobody won any reasonable amount and yet nursed hope of winning and so continued to spend in the betting game until irredeemably impoverished. I really did not see anybody playing Pools that was rich. I knew a very close relative of my wife who was a Pools Agent. He had an office in eternally congested McIver Road in Warri with two chalked boards by the door where betters came on Saturday evenings to check whether they had won or not. One board had a list of English teams and the other board Australian teams. Each board was marked with Xs and 0s, a sort of tic-tac-toe. I overheard players always coming so close to winning without ever winning and that spurred them to continue betting on teams so far away from their reality. I heard of Everton, Hull, Liverpool, and some others. My wife's relation "played Pools" until his office closed when his wife raised a commotion by the Pools Centre in McIver Road that he should spend his money to feed his family rather than spend on phantom players. The public embarrassment cured him of his addiction. I also knew a police officer in Maiduguri who was a compulsive Pools player. Rumors had it that he took so much bribes to squander on his addiction and retired poor. So my experience as a young man of English Football was of gambling.

But things have changed. The European world has a way of reinventing itself. With globalization, things have taken a new turn. The football organizers get to your pocket through your heart. These engines of globalization compel you to subscribe to DSTV from South Africa for Super Sports channel. Individual homes, hotels, university offices, and many others subscribe to the sports channel to watch English Premier League or European Football. Many men have the time to watch sports and no time to read or do productive things for themselves or their families. Nigerians have joined European rival football clubs. Many households and offices have their different clubs they cheer on. I saw Nigerian professors fly flags of their English or European teams without shame. Families are split on European football club sides. I know of a house in which the wife and the kids are Chelsea fans and the man a Manchester United fan. Whenever the two teams met, the house was so divided that a civil war broke out. The man jokingly told me that when Manchester defeated Chelsea, he did not expect sex that night since the woman would be so dejected, depressed, and unresponsive as not to be interested in anything with him. He told me that he had tried to pay back if Chelsea beat Manchester United! Theirs was good tit for tat.

Watching television news, especially Channels' sports programs or listening to the FM stations, I often marveled at the knowledge of the commentators. The same with what I will call common folks in the street or you meet in barber shops and other places. They know the players very well; they know their histories, their transfer records, and so much that qualify them as experts in English or European football. The European teams have African/Nigerian players that even drive the audience ratings of their matches because Nigerians identify with some of the players. This fetches so much money for the teams and the television, especially DSTV. Nigerians watch the matches while Europe and South Africa reap the financial rewards. The irony of it is that the same Nigerians who talk so knowledgeably about European clubs and players know very little about their local clubs. Doubtless they will say that the league system is not developed in Nigeria, but it is left for them to develop it. In South Africa and Egypt it appears there is national interest in their football clubs. I was in South Africa from the first to about the third week of April and there was national excitement as the Bafana Bafana Boys played their rivals.

I went to play ping pong with Jude the day that Arsenal and Hull played the English F.A. Cup Final. After we had finished playing, Jude winning more games than I did, we went to the lounge to watch the clash of the English Titans, so to say. The lounge was packed full because there were many large screen televisions around and there was constant light. Many of the Club members came to watch with their guests. I had no favorite club but Jude was for Arsenal. Other members were either for Arsenal or Hull. I, as normal with me, then took the side of the underdog for this match because it seemed the experts had chosen Arsenal over Hull. I think within the first thirty minutes Hull scored a goal and there was jubilation as the Arsenal fans turned glum. An altercation arose in which one of the Arsenal fans stood up before everybody, almost punching the jubilating Hull fans.

"I am ready to die for Arsenal," he started shouting.

This was a man who looked cowardly and would not step forward to die for anything Nigerian. I would write a poem that night.

Let Them Die For Arsenal
"I am ready to die for Arsenal" (Nigerian fan as Arsenal played Hull City on May 17, 2014 in the days of *Bringbackourgirls*)

Let them die for Arsenal
and millions more for Chelsea, Manchu, and Real Madrid
those who hide as neighbors die from armed robbery
those who do nothing seeing their property carted away
those who watch their mothers, wives, and daughters raped
those who pay phantom light bills for blackout months
those whose reps steal their share of the national wealth

those who abandon their children in war to save themselves
those who flee rather than club to death the cobra at the
doorstep.

Let them die for Arsenal
those who raise not arms against brutish police and soldiers
those who choose to accept kola rather than simple truth
those who "hammer" rather than live on honest hard work
those who stop not after a perilous pothole to plant a red flag
those who refuse to be eyes of the blind and feet of the
crippled
those who sell body parts to build mansions they won't live in
those defecating daily on their parents' marked graves
those who abandon fellow travelers involved in ghastly
accidents.

Let them die for Arsenal
die for Arsenal, die for all the Europa clubs
and let the strong breed here live on
die for Arsenal and rid the land of a contagion
die for Arsenal and rid the land of psychos and suicides
die for Arsenal, die for Chelsea and avert a national implosion
die for Arsenal, die for Manchu and rid the streets of loose
cannons
die for Arsenal, die for Real Madrid and rid the neighborhood
of rot
die for Arsenal, die for Ajax and rid the state of fifth
columnists.

Let them die for Arsenal
die for a white-robed masquerade
die for a tall hat trick
die for the golden rule of sudden death
die for a stealth hard shot
die for a coconut header

die for an assist ball
die for dirty passes
die for hitting the ball hard.

Die for Arsenal
die not from Holy Ghost fire
die not from the menace of witchcraft
die not from kicking an empty bucket
die not from a poisonous snakebite
die not from a motor crash
die not from defending the handicapped against abusers
die not from a massive heart attack
die, die, die for Arsenal.

You don't die for many causes
you don't die for Arsenal and still die for Nigeria
you die for only one cause
you don't die for Arsenal and still bring back our stolen
children
there's only one death
die for Arsenal and you are gone as a person
you have only one life
throw it away for Arsenal and desecrate your homeland
die for Arsenal.

Die for Arsenal, my king of fools
die for Arsenal, my retarded brother
die for Arsenal, my homeless relative
die for Arsenal whose body will be carcass for vultures
die for Arsenal, whose body won't be buried in England
die for Arsenal, stray rabid dog
die for Arsenal, my compatriot
die for Arsenal who will not die for God
let them all die for Arsenal.

I observe the popularity of Africa Magic as workers in offices in many universities and government offices have it tuned on permanently. At Amassoma, I observe that the cafeteria workers are more interested in Africa Magic than serving people food. At most hotels in Abuja and Warri, among other places, the workers ignore guests because they are possessed by Africa Magic. This is the home video entertainment to which so many people are addicted. I support Nollywood but that should not mean that I should abandon the work for which I am paid to watch television.

I think by far the Nigerian understanding of recreation comes down to drinking spots where you can drink beer or whatever else (wine or soft drinks) and have barbecued fish, suya, isi-ewu, and other delicacies. It is so popular that men and women go either in company or on their own. From my visit to Taraba among the Mumuye women, the Birom of Jos, and others, this is a great recreation for Nigerians. At Yola there is a fish joint and my friend Ola told me that once one ate the fish there, one was bound to return. I had returned there two years after first eating at the fish joint, and won't mind if there is peace there to go back for more. Abuja has so many of such joints in the Wuse II, Garki, by Crystal Palace Hotel, and other areas. You pick the live fish that you want and it is barbecued for you. There are many such joints in the Effurun-Warri area and I think the most popular is the PTI Staff Club one where on weekends the place is filled with hundreds of fun lovers. In Effurun, Warri, Ughelli, Agbarho, and elsewhere around such drinking places are hot spots for friends, lovers or partners who want to socialize together.

It appears Nigerians are drinking more than before and that appeals to their concept of relaxation. I thought about it and came to the conclusion that people really needed avenues for relaxation and that was all they could get. On another level, it could be that it is a means of self-denial of their precarious condition and a device to suppress the stress which seems to have a stranglehold over so many. Ironically, by drinking, they increase the precarious condition, since they spend money that could be used for food at home or educating their children. Many drinkers exacerbate their health conditions such as diabetes and hypertension. By overeating and taking alcohol or sugary drinks, they constitute a health hazard to themselves in the name of going out to relax.

9

THE IRRESISTIBLE ALLURE OF MONEY

Money has an irresistible allure in Nigeria where the people live as in a land of spirits. Most Nigerians spend far more than their salaries or incomes can afford. Where do men and women get money from outside their salaries or legitimate incomes to live beyond their means? As a friend told me in Abuja, "men are thieves and women prostitutes." While this may be a hyperbole but it speaks to the truth of the situation. Money has become a god. It confers power on those who have it. It confers respect on those who amass so much of it that it becomes ludicrous. With it one can get one's desire. As it is said in some parts of Nigeria, with money Satan can arrange to smuggle himself into heaven. That is, if God were a Nigerian! But fortunately, He is not. Or if heaven were Nigeria! And fortunately too, it is not.

For its importance money is universally idolized. Everybody seeks it. Pastors and priests seek it. Presidents seek it. Wives of presidents seek it. The sick seek it. The terminally ill seek it. The poor seek it. It appears nobody feels he or she has got enough money (even when rich) and the seeking continues with intensity. One Urhobo singer, I believe Okpa Aribo, created a myth about this unending seeking of money. Money was a boy entrusted in the hands of some adults who went out but soon lost him when they digressed to do some other things. Ever since then, they had to search for Igho (Money) and have up till now not found him (it!). Even when they find Igho, they are not satisfied that they have found him. And so it has become a lifelong search that consumes everyone.

If money were guarded by death, many would still try to overpower death to snatch it! As a young unemployed young man told me in Warri, better to try to step over death to seek money than not try! His reasoning was that whether you confront death or not over money, you are going to die anyway! "No try, no fail," he said, using the local saying.

To many folks, money is a god to be sacrificed to. I will come back later to the narrative of rituals to make money. Folks betray others, sacrificing love and friendship, to make money. Similarly, many people betray relatives in their efforts to seek money. Many sacrifice truth for the sake of money. Honesty can fall victim in the pursuit of money. Loyalty too can fall victim to the love of money. It is difficult to be ethically and morally upright and be rich in Nigeria. The desire for money benumbs the conscience. And this covers not just government workers but also those who bribe or lobby for oil blocs, businessmen and women who lobby for state contracts they do not execute and set money aside for kickbacks to those who gave them the contracts. The inordinate greed has infected workers from the top to the bottom. There are those who take their department's budgets as personal funds. People cut corners either to be rich or make both ends meet in Nigeria. I was told about a Professor who was given a political appointment and who boasted that generations of his family would not need to work again to live well all their lives! And he said that, confident of the money he had amassed in a few years of service. That boast typifies the deeply corrupt public servant. Others sell their souls to make money and later die like vultures.

"Money makes iron float," many Nigerians say. Of course, only in Nigerian waters can iron float. "Without money, you are nothing," many others say to justify their foul methods of making money. As I learnt, there are many ready to do more daring things than stepping over death to reach money. Some will attempt to snatch money from the jaws of death to be rich. I have heard that some policemen at accident scenes first search and empty the pockets and purses of the dead victims before taking them to the morgue. Many will do all they think they can to defy death and seize the money even if it is in death's safe! I wish they had a little more brain to think wisely or know they came to this world empty-handed and would leave also empty-handed. Who knows? Many of the Nigerian super rich through corruption might be thinking they would carry their assets to the afterworld. Too much money is capable of causing self-delusion about one's abilities and expectations.

From my people's names, one can see how money is idolized. It is worshiped more than the Almighty in their names and sayings. Etaredaferua—the rich person's talk is listened to. My own father's name, Dafetanure, is part of this folklore of wealth. It means the rich have spoken! And it implies that the poor or the rest of the populace will have to concur and remain silent! Another name, Ighorhiohwunu, means money empowers one to speak out. Edafiagho—it is the rich who are respected. Igho she mu whe—money makes doing things possible! Yes, it makes many things possible but not everything. Another common saying is "Ako mre igho ko whe"—the teeth see money and begin to laugh. In other words, money brings laughter. Recently, I argued with acquaintances at the Petroleum Training Institute's Staff Club about the power of money to change humans. Many believe money can make you respected and honored. I believe this happens as they have observed in Nigeria. The academic and non-academic staff of the Petroleum Training Institute, Effurun, is made up of people from different parts of Nigeria, and so their observations are very telling. There is the human character that confers respect and honor whether or not one is rich or poor. What one does with money is important. To me, money should be used to resolve one's or others' problems. There is a litany of ways in which money confers social status on one, according to traditional lore. I can only agree it is only to some extent. I believe most groups in Nigeria have such names and sayings as the Urhobo that idolize money. It seems to me that the greed for money has been increasing over the decades but has now reached a maniacal stage. What has brought this about?

Globalization has intensified the greed for money because it whets appetites for luxury goods and gadgets that are promoted in the regular and social media. These expensive articles are imported and people crave for them. Nigerians are avid consumers of what others produce and so there is an array of foreign produce and products in stores. I don't know where the apples consumed in Nigeria come from in Europe, France or Poland, but it is an industry of billions of naira. Some folks go to Benin Republic to buy apples and frozen chicken and turkey to sell in Nigeria. I heard that it appeared some of the poultry meat was preserved with the same chemicals used for embalming corpses. Apples are available now in some of the remotest villages and towns in Nigeria. Of course, they are waxed with chemicals to preserve and make them look fresh. With apples coming from Europe, there appears to be no incentive planting apples in Plateau and Taraba States that could grow them.

Globalization has brought cell phones and there are millions of subscribers. Many Nigerians carry three to four cellphones (often called mobile phones) and subscribe to different networks since they trust none in efficiency. When Airtel is not working well, maybe MTN or Glow or Etisalat or Visa might be working. Depending upon where you live, some networks have poor reception perennially. For a long time I thought it was crazy having more than one phone and resisted having another phone. Then came a period in which MTN on which I placed so much trust was not working for days and I had to have an Airtel line.

"You can see what I have been telling you," a junior colleague told me.

"I understand now why many folks carry many phones," I replied.

"I am happy you are now absorbing the Nigerian experience," she said, laughing.

I still find it odd for one person to carry four phones. I know one or two Nigerian colleagues who vowed not to have more than one phone. Later one of them bought a two-some phone that carried two SIM cards from different networks but only one can operate at a time and each with its own ring tone.

Since most Nigerians like gadgets, they go for expensive phones. They are always conscious of the latest phones in BlackBerry, Samsung, Galaxies, I-Phones, and others. Younger folks, boys and girls, and women generally tend to go for the latest versions of these phones which are very expensive. Older folks have to indulge themselves and their families in many more ways. Friends, especially female ones, mocked me for having an antiquated Nokia phone they described as "Stone Me." It was a basic phone that was strong and ironically picked towns and villages which I passed when traveling but which my friends' smart phones did not. Its GPS worked. I later misplaced the phone somewhere and never got it again. I don't know whether any of my friends asking me to "throw it away" really threw it away. I bought a more expensive phone which I feel is not giving me as much service and peace of mind as the lost one.

In addition to having expensive phones, people, especially the young, want all the features and apps available to be current with the world. These phones, I-Pads, and other tablets cost so much money outside the developed world in which they are manufactured. Many parents now buy tablets and other gadgets for their children expanding their purchasing horizon which they have to reach with money. One is not surprised at the busy and crowded stores such as SLOT on Airport Road, Effurun, or the many stores of the Robinson Plaza on Deco Road in Warri.

In the universities, one sees girls with very expensive phones and sometimes two or three of different brands. In my compound in Effurun, a young man who was unemployed had I-Phone, Samsung, and Android phones. That was thanks to his indulging mother! Other young men and women had been "blessed" by parents or some *mugu* and they rushed to buy their fantasy phones. The desire to buy a phone of their dreams could make many young men and women seek money in extraordinary ways.

I understand that while the cellphone companies give free recharge cards to legislators at state and federal levels, the ordinary people pay for what has been given free to the political elites. Nigerian domestic calls are some of the most expensive in the entire world. Why should those who earn so much money be given free phone cards? It is a bribe to stop them from lowering tariffs for the generality of the populace. This would be unacceptable in most countries of the world and would be seen as a political scandal. But Nigerians are programmed to accept unpopular measures even when exploited as in this case.

I saw an old friend of mine after almost thirty-five years. We were friends in our twenties but have piled years over our ages since then. As is said, we had both gone on our own ways. I could barely recognize the slim figure with a wasp's waist in the new madam I saw. She reminded me that she had "dropped four engines," meaning she had delivered four times. In any case, we were happy to meet again and joked a bit about the old days. Kemi told me that she was addicted to phoning and would rather buy recharge cards for her three phones than buy medicine for her fever, which could be malaria or typhoid! She had told me she was feverish and I asked her to take care of herself. Since she was adamant about buying recharge cards before any other thing that even involves her health, I stopped at a pharmacy to buy her malaria drugs. As I paid for the drugs, she bought recharge cards double the cost of the malaria and typhoid drugs and Vitamin C that I paid for! I played the *mugu* by saving her money for her to indulge in her phoning frenzy though sick. I told another friend of mine who condemned what I did.

"Did you want me to leave her to be sick or die?" I asked.

"How would she change, if she can have somebody like you to always pity her by not forcing her to spend her money on her health?"

"OK, I made a mistake," I said, "but still I can't carry my outrage that far as not to care for an ignorant person's health," I explained.

I took in the query and should I be in Kemi's company again, I would not assist her in pursuing her being possessed by the god of mobile phones.

Many Nigerians are on Face Book and other social media and it costs money to have regular Internet connection. But that is only the communication aspect.

More than before Nigerians are taking vacations in the United States, Europe, United Arab Emirate, South Africa, and other places. This means much more money to be spent. Women want to wear the most fashionable clothes and shoes sold in London, Paris, New York, and Milan that many of them cannot afford with their earnings. One female lecturer boasts to me she does not use local handbags. "How will I use them when Gucci and other brands are there?" she asked me. While in Bellagio many years ago, I remember trying to pick a Gucci bag for my wife and the Italian shopkeeper told me, "If you want a Gucci, you have to spend a lot of money" in that seductive Italian accent. A Nigerian who wants to wear brand names has to spend a lot of money! Many Nigerians want to go shopping in Dubai, India, Switzerland, Turkey, and China, among so many countries. Men want to build mansions and buy beautiful cars to show off that they have "arrived." I have heard that some folks build gigantic mansions but would not even sleep in them! Men want to be manly by being unnecessarily generous to those who will praise them to massage their egos. And many will steal to please or pamper women they fancy. Money has cast a maniacal spell over almost everybody.

In addition to the seductive products of globalization, Nigerians I interacted with or lived among during the more than one year had many social pressures to bow to and in so doing incur expenses that stretch them beyond their earned salaries. There are social and other meetings to host. One is not an island, I often hear, and so many people are members of one social association or another. There could be town meetings in the city to continue bonding with one's townsmen or women. Some are purely social as some women's groups in Warri—Elegant Women's Club and Ufuoma Women's Club. Others have church groups to host. I remember a friend of mine who is a Knight of Mulumba and another friend a Knight of St. John. My Catholic friends and their fellow knights host each other on a rotating basis and have to prepare food and buy cartons of drinks to entertain themselves as Christian brethren. Their wives do most of the task of the hosting. The hosting of meetings or other groups involves buying expensive clothes to wear on occasions together with the entertainments. Often members go and "greet" their members when bereaved, celebrating births, weddings, promotions, and other things to show solidarity and flaunt their social standing in society. This by itself is a manifestation of the traditional collective spirit of Africans and I remember John Mbiti's words I tell my students: "I am because we are." Yes, I am because we are, but these social groups exact a financial and psychological toll on members. Oftentimes men and women face physical and psychological stress in trying to meet their responsibilities as members of many associations. Many try to out-do the previous group that hosted and I have heard of members borrowing money to host fellow members of a society. How will members of these groups not seek money with a vengeance?

How will Nigerians not make money at all cost, even if they have to "hammer"? By "hammer," I mean jumping at every opportunity without qualms to make a lot of money. One has to be prepared at all times for unexpected expenditures. If the government officials fall sick, they are airlifted to Germany, France, Saudi Arabia, and elsewhere for treatment. For others, workers and the nouveau riches, it is a matter of "God for us all and I for myself!" The hospitals in Nigeria are not well equipped with tools and doctors to serve the teeming population and people die needlessly. Most of the deaths in Nigeria are preventable, a medical doctor friend of mine told me. I agree with him. Nothing has come out of the National Health Scheme announced with fanfare some time ago. At 3Js Hotel where I stayed for some days while in Abuja, I saw ahead from the hotel gate the headquarters of the National Health Scheme. I took a walk to the building and it was all civil servants and no health there, I felt. Many sick Nigerians who have the means now flock to India for treatment. Many others go to South Africa, Saudi Arabia, Britain, and the United States, among so many destinations.

I happened to go to the Indian High Commission, Abuja, for a visa to attend the Sahitya Akademi's World Poetry Festival in New Delhi. The first morning that I was there at about 8:50 in the morning, the gate for those seeking Indian visa to be interviewed had just closed, I learnt. I went too late. The following morning, I had to be there at 6:30 a.m. for the gate to be opened at 8:30 a.m. I saw the crowd of mainly middle-aged men and women and, apart from me and a student, all those applying for Indian visa wanted to travel there for medical reasons. I happened to be the second person on the queue. However, the man in my front and I were called at the same time to come to the table in an open space inside. Fortunately, since I was officially invited by the Indian Ministry of Culture, I was told to go in to pay the visa fee and submit my passport to another official in another room. By the time I was going in to pay, a large crowd was already in, since the gate has closed for more visa applicants to enter that day.

As I sat in the room waiting to be attended to, I could hear shouts of people complaining about being told to bring proof that they were really going to India for medical treatment. About ten minutes passed. Then some shrill wailing came from those waiting outside. A man had collapsed. The two Indian officials interviewing the visa applicants left the table and were making frantic phone calls to remove the dead or dying man. Later I understood that the man had come daily the past three days for a visa to go to India for an undisclosed but seemingly terminal ailment. The man and his wife were put in a taxi and waved away from the Indian High Commission! By the time I was leaving only one other person who had prepaid for the hospital treatment with a receipt had got a visa to travel to India. In any case, whatever the destination, it is huge sums of money in foreign exchange taken to be spent for treatment outside.

One of the new trends in Nigeria is hearing parents boast of the schools that their children attend. For us who had attended the government-run schools, we seem outdated. The vogue is to send one's children to private schools—from elementary through secondary to the university. Those whose salaries or earnings would not be enough for the exorbitant fees charged or who would be hard pressed still have to send their children to private schools by all means.

"I can't send my children to those rickety government schools," a friend told me.

"But you and I attended them and we are not doing poorly," I told him.

"Yes, that was in those days. The children of these poor people do not create a good atmosphere for serious children to learn," he said.

I was surprised. So, being a son or daughter of a poor person makes one not behave well. I had thought the children of rich folks are spoilt and cause problems for the rest of their schoolmates. In any case, it has become a class thing to send children to school and so every parent wants to do so and has to seek money to do so. My sister sends her children in Port Harcourt to private schools from elementary to secondary schools. Her husband doesn't have a job and her retail business in the market is not doing well because she needs money to boost the trade. My friends' children all go to private schools at the elementary and secondary school levels. The daughter of my co-in-law's children go to the American University in Nigeria in Yola and a daughter is studying medicine at Igbenedion University in Benin, both of which pay extremely high fees. The private universities are very expensive and in Abuja both Bazc University and Turkish-Nile University charge a fee as much as three million naira (about eighteen thousand US dollars) per year. Nigerians need money to meet their parental demands of sending their children to private schools in Nigeria or overseas to study. My friend Dr. Jonathan has told me of a veterinary doctor who sends his children to two private universities in Nigeria. His real salary is not more than three hundred thousand naira (about two thousand US dollars) a month. This man has schemed to be not only the vet doctor of the farm but also its manager and chief accountant. The big poultry farm has almost collapsed and one does not need to probe to tell where the profits of the farm go to. The manager's two children in expensive private universities have to be funded!

There are chieftaincy titles to take and spend lavishly upon for empty titles to boost one's ego in a society that likes titles. My mentor, Chief Dickson Onojegbe is the Osiolele of Ughelli Kingdom. From his chieftaincy title, he draws upon himself money, children, and good health. He tells me it takes up to five million naira (about thirty thousand US dollars) to be an Ughelli chief. I know that in some Urhobo clans or kingdoms it could cost as little as only five thousand naira, but for most institutions it costs far higher for what would not improve the quality of lives of the title holders other than varnish their vanity. This ostentatious practice drives some folks to seek money to be counted among the chiefs of their areas.

There are also weddings and burial ceremonies that need so much money to fund. In fact, in some parts of the Delta, many "celebrants" at burial ceremonies want to create a record at entertaining guests or break existing records of spending. The folly of it is that people spend more money at funerals than they would voluntarily give out to assist anyone to go to the hospital or solve a simple financial problem. My people have invented ways now of spending lavishly money they don't really have by having introduction, traditional marriage (bride-price paying ceremony), and so-called "white wedding." Young men borrow what it would take them a decade to pay back just to be seen as great celebrants. Thinking of the mentality of breaking records in entertaining or spending money, I remember my Grandma's saying. She told me: "If you do a burial ceremony and everybody praises you for entertaining so well, then you are a fool." There are many fools in my Delta area and elsewhere in Nigeria where many spend absurd amounts of money at burial ceremonies. These fools, by my Grandma's reckoning, seek money by all means to massage their egos to be seen as rich or doing well but everything comes at a big cost.

To make money, many Nigerians take to illicit actions. Generally, in the country, there is kidnaping in the East and South-South; ritual killings to make money in the West; and baby factories in the East and the eastern section of the South-South. Armed robbery, kidnaping, ritual killings, and operating baby factories result from the maniacal greed for money. Some folks have now come to the inevitable decision in a money-crazy land that they have to make money by all means necessary. By foul means, of course! I had had my

colleagues and friends advise me to be very careful because of
kidnapers. But, like the popular song says, "Be careful, be
careful, how careful can I be? I don't know the person who
will do me in." A junior colleague at Abraka was particularly
concerned about my security, since knowing I am an America-
based professor and that information would jeopardize my
safety. I tried as much as I could to be security-conscious. I
dressed as simply as I could and stopped my walking in
neighboring streets and instead drove to the Petroleum
Training Institute campus to walk and drive back. The fear of
being a target of the money-hungry changes one's lifestyle in
Nigeria.

     Kidnaping was reported almost all the time
everywhere. It struck close when the junior colleague herself
was kidnaped. She went through a ten-day ordeal before her
release for which a hefty amount might have been paid. The
kidnaping gangs demand ransoms of forty million naira,
depending on how they assess their victims' worth. What
started in the Niger Delta as part of a resource control struggle
in the kidnaping of Shell's expatriate workers later developed
into ransom demands in the eastern part of Nigeria; Aba
became notorious and feared for its kidnaping gangs. They
worked with armed robbers who also want money at all cost,
even if they have to kill stubborn victims not ready to
surrender money. So many Nigerians were ready to go to any
length to make money to be seen as rich and take care of what
they fancy.

     Bad as armed robbery and kidnaping are, even worse
are the thriving baby-making factories in some parts of the
country, especially in the East and a few states in the South-
South region. During my stay in Nigeria, especially the early
part of 2014, there was often news of police arresting owners
of baby factories where young women were paid to have
babies that would be taken away from them for rituals to make
money or reinforce politicians to win elections or stay in

power. I heard from public rumor that some big politicians might be using such babies for rituals to be acquitted of serious legal cases. As I drove through the Otokutu Bridge on the Delta Steel Complex Road near Warri, a passenger pointed at a spot where human body parts used to be sold under the bridge to secret buyers that came from far and near to make medicines for money or political careers. The greed for money by the killers of such people whose body parts were on sale and the buyers is horrendous.

Twice towards the end of my stay in Nigeria, there were news items of ritual murders in the West and the Delta. In the two Western areas, including an Ibadan forest, skeletons of victims used for rituals were found. In an extreme case in the Delta, a chap was kidnaped and, even after the ransom was paid for his freedom, the corpse was found with the tongue, manhood, liver, and other internal organs removed. There was so much news about a shrine in a university town in the East where human sacrifice was suspected to be performed. I understand that Abuja and Asaba, among so many other administrative centers, have the largest concentration of marabouts, dibias, babalawos, and medicine-men in the country. I understand that there are marabouts from the Sudan and Mali in the Abuja area. So much is the demand for medicines that the medicine men now ask for their fees to be paid in foreign exchange—dollars, pounds, and euros. While at Abuja, I heard of a medicine man who asked for a gallon of human blood to perform rituals of perpetual power or money-doubling for politicians.

People want to get rich or want to seek political offices with diabolic means and then make so much money. One scenario of the money-making, they say, involves invoking money through the skull used to make the medicine and money fell from it. Since there is one thousand naira denomination, there should be a flow of the thousand naira bill. I am not surprised that some rich Nigerians, who are supposed to be economists and know that with the high denomination inflation would go up, still campaigned for a five-thousand naira denomination! Their money-doubling skulls would have made them five times richer than they would be at the current time. Such experts have not studied why the American dollar's highest denomination has remained $100 and the British pound 50. It is not the higher the denomination, the stronger the currency. Or even the more the currency denomination, the richer the country. Thieves could easily be blind-sighted to think that the more the better!

The stampede to amass wealth by fair or foul means is so strong that under my nose in Warri or Abuja, I was told there were so many new cults. So-called secret societies whose meeting places at Eku and Ginuwa Road, Warri, I knew as a boy, were visible to the public. Not so, these new ones which are stronger and said to promote and protect members. Now I am told there is a Zaki cult but don't have information about it. There is another with an ethnic name Gbejugbele, literally meaning "I don't listen!" if its laws are violated by sworn members. I am told at Warri that there were many young men and women who joined to be successful in business, a euphemism for "getting rich quick" by whatever means. An older man told me to read obituaries and see that many young men die at the age of fifty. From his explanation, new initiates into cults were promised wealth but had to pay with their lives when fifty. One would expect such people to be afraid and desist from what they were offered. But so strong is the desire for money that they brush aside fear and accept wealth with all its consequences. Money has become so tempting that it may now be possible for some Nigerians, if given the chance, to sell their mothers for rituals to make money!

In any country where money assumes so much importance, morality and ethics are thrown to dogs. There is so much dishonesty and scheming to exploit and cheat others for one's benefit. The term 419 has been in Nigeria for a long time; its current usage taken from the criminal code handbook for fraudulent extortion. Many young men are using the Internet to their negative advantage. I had almost been a victim once while in the United States of this fraud. That was some eight years ago. Someone had telephoned me from Lagos.

"Bruce Onobrakpeya is in the hospital. He has been involved in an accident and he is in a very critical condition. We need money for blood and his treatment and he needs you to deposit five hundred thousand naira before we can continue the treatment. Send the money through Western Union immediately."

I was surprised that the speaker had my number and wondered how he knew my relationship with the Owena, our foremost visual artist.

"It is very urgent," the conman doctor's voice from across the ocean warned.

I would not allow anything to happen to Bruce because of that amount, even if I had to borrow it. A quick idea came to my mind. Why shouldn't I call the Owena's daughter, who was then a student in Virginia? I called her.

"Are you sure it is not 419?" she asked me, after I told her about the telephone call I had just received from Lagos.

"I don't know," I said.

"You can't pay that money without any of us reaching our mother first," she demanded.

"OK," I replied.

Within ten minutes, she called back. "I talked to my dad and mom. They are fine at home. That call should be a 419. Just ignore the person," she told me.

When the doctor conman in Lagos called back, I told him, "You conman and scam artist, I am going to give your number to the police to arrest you."

He dropped the phone.

There are the Yahoo boys and perhaps girls. While the most advanced ones have their own laptops and operate from their rooms or solitary places, the younger ones operate from cybercafés where I went once in a while to access my UNC Charlotte emails that for some reasons I couldn't open at home in my laptop. Anytime I was in one of those cybercafés you can overhear the boys on the phone and at the same time surfing. They seem to be talking to a fellow Nigerian con artist and online on the Yahoo Messenger or something else with their foreign victims.

"She has agreed to send five hundred dollars," the Yahoo boy tells his fellow scammer.

"Can't you flatter her to send a thousand dollars? Tell her, 'Sweet darling, I love you so so much. You are sweeter than any sweet thing anybody can think of. I will make you wow when I touch you when I come.' Tell her that," the more seasoned crook at home counselled.

"I go try. No try, no fail," he replied, as he dropped the phone to execute the tricks he had learnt from his senior.

They convert the stuffy cybercafé into a chat room for nefarious acts. "No try, no fail" for the sake of money. I saw young men who were ostensibly unemployed driving fairly good used cars and, I understand, have good cash in their bank accounts. Effurun and Warri can boast of many of the Yahoo boys. They are sharp generally and I only wonder why some women so lonely in the United States or Canada will start a liaison with these devils. Loneliness and lack of love could drive some people to be easy prey for such predators.

I had money sent to me through MoneyGram several times while on my fellowship. I spent more money while in Nigeria than in the United States. I had two generators which broke down as soon as serviced and I paid exorbitant charges to have them working again. My impression is that these gen repairers do not really know what they are doing and through trial so many times may get it right once. I had to buy fuel at so-called black market prices during frequent fuel scarcities, since I chose not to spend half a day or more queueing for petrol when I could do something else more productive. I spent money on the plumbing of my house and had plumbers who also charged exorbitantly without getting right what they were doing. The repairers often asked you to give them money for spare parts for the repair jobs and only God knows the actual cost of what they bought. Sometimes I suspected they did not buy anything but I was helpless before them. Even when they bought things, one could not trust the quality of what they bought and there was no change brought back to you.

There were so many ways to spend money unexpectedly in Nigeria. The point I am making is that it is very expensive to live well in Nigeria and I am not surprised that those whose earnings are modest or low have to scheme for other ways to make money to cope with the Joneses! It is not easy to pretend that one has money if one doesn't have it. It is what you wear, drive, where you live, and how you live that will indicate your standard of living. In Nigeria most people need far more than their modest salaries to cope with the luxuries that modernity and globalization have made more alluring and irresistible.

I witnessed one case of an American immigrant coming back to Nigeria to see the house he had been sending so much money home to his senior brother to build for him. It is a common phenomenon that many Nigerians in the United States have been aware of through personal experience.

"My brother has duped me," Chris complained.

"What prevented you from coming all these years to do what you want to do yourself?" I asked him.

"I thought as my brother, and my senior for that matter, that he would do it wholeheartedly!" he said with exasperation.

Wholeheartedly, I mused. Money is so seductive that it breaks relationships with brothers, sisters, cousins, uncles and aunts, and a few cases of children and their parents. I pitied

Chris who sent so much money through Western Union as if he did not work for money but plucked dollar bills from trees in his backyard.

At the banks all of which now take part in the Western Union and MoneyGram money transfers, I see young and old women and young men, perhaps the scammers, crowding the section waiting for their transfers to be processed. Wherever money is processed in Nigeria, expect it to be crowded. I find those who send money to their relatives and friends in Nigeria from abroad commendable in not forgetting their homes and the relationships they have struck. Much as they are on the receiving end, I also commend the Nigerians who have maintained their relationships with relatives and friends abroad. It takes two sides to maintain such bonds. Money can bring out the good and the bad in a people and reciprocal relationships matter a lot.

I observed how things seemed to have changed in many ways since when I first worked in Effurun and now. Most young people in Effurun and Warri I sent on errands now did not bring back any change to me unless I asked for the change. Far back in the past, it was different. With the exception of Ebruvwiyor, who returned change anytime I sent him to buy me things, the others took it as an entitlement to hold on to the change they got as their reward. "Nothing goes for nothing," they say in the Effurun-Warri area.

The greed for money is costing us honesty and a good name. I saw no coins in Nigeria, unlike either in the United States or the three countries I visited while still doing my fellowship in Nigeria. Why the Nigerian Government does not see the wisdom of having coins in a decimalized currency, I don't know. When one buys anything, be it food, fuel, medicine, or whatever, and the total falls short of five naira, there is usually no change. What I found most unusual is that it is the seller who tells you there is no change and wants to keep the money that is owed you the buyer. I believe at the petrol station, the attendant deliberately stops the pump at an amount that will give her some naira that he or she will not give to the customer. Done to so many drivers who stop by to buy fuel, the attendant could make so much money at the end of the day. It is a form of extortion.

In the midst of many swindlers and duplicitous men and women who seek money by all means necessary, there are many exceptions. I have met some men and women who refuse to do the wrong thing in accepting bribes and helping folks on their own merits. Some who work in offices have been maligned by the bad guys and transferred from such offices where they were trying to inculcate probity on their fellow workers. I know three cases that I need to mention as shining examples of people who may want money but not through corrupt means. One, a woman, headed a department and she wanted those qualified to be employed. In so doing, the others felt she was depriving them from making money and plotted to bribe her boss, the Director, to have her transferred from Lagos to Abuja, where she would have to rent an expensive apartment and be shuttling to Lagos to see her husband and children on weekends. She accepted the transfer without complaint and knowing that she had to make a sacrifice for her probity. Another example, a man, a military marched the person who brought a big Ghana-must-go bag filled with naira to him for a favor. Many officers would have smiled and thanked God for the bribe; some officers would even have saluted a *bloody civilian* for the blessing.

A third person whose self-restraint about money I want to praise is a Federal Ministry official who works in a lucrative department in the Ministry of Lands and Housing. He was transferred to a department and the person who had been there and posted away refused to leave because he could not afford, according to him, to leave his desk. The officer transferred there told their Permanent Secretary that he wanted to work and be paid and so did not want a lucrative desk. He was given another desk. Though the fellow workers saw him as a fool, he told me he preferred his peace to anything that would bring him evil money. There are many others in the universities, state and federal ministries, parastatals, and other organizations that are not seduced by money. But these are the exceptions and so are unlike the mass of the populace and that gladdens my heart.

10

THE LOVE OF CEREMONIES IS THE SECRET OF HAPPINESS

Despite the apparent misery an outsider perceives among Nigerians, that observation is contradicted by the many social gatherings, weddings, burials, and other parties that take place weekly. At least that is the way I saw things from my residence in the Effurun area as I saw Urhobo, Itsekiri, Isoko, Ijo, Bini, Yoruba, and Igbo folks involved in ceremonies and parties. Nigerians are generally a happy people. Or put differently, Nigerians display a sense of happiness in many ceremonies and parties that belie the economic struggles and the existential fear of diabolic forces they might be facing. I always told a friend in Warri that the people around were doing very well; they might not be rich but have enough money to buy beautiful clothes and organize fabulous parties and provide great entertainment. He made me believe that people are struggling but also know that they have only one life to live. I agreed with him. Among my Agbon clansmen and women, the saying that "Ariosa se ibi" (You borrow to make a grand impression), is very popular. You borrow to throw a big party to entertain the public and after the event you work hard to pay back the debts you may have incurred to make the grand impression! I think many Nigerians, especially in the Niger Delta area, live by this philosophy. Take care of now and let the future take care of itself!

Being a Niger Delta person and a Nigerian, I am bound to get invited to many ceremonies. Almost on a weekly basis, there are burial ceremonies and weddings. At other times there are other parties, including chieftaincy installations, thanksgiving, and naming ceremonies. There are many burial ceremonies. I don't know whether because death is treated more clinically in the United States, but one sees death as a daily, if not weekly, presence in Nigeria. In the United States, the institution of homes takes the very old out of sight and their deaths in homes or hospitals would not be noticed. Also when somebody sick is seen as irreversibly gone, he or she is taken to a hospice to spend the last several days before expiring. Again, the person is carefully taken out of public sight. The burial/memorial service, interment, and refreshments are often of a low key compared to the fanfare in the Nigerian death and burial I witness. It is not that things have changed so much in Nigeria but the style has become standard. It is a means of showing off one's wealth or social status.

Past are the days when "wake keeping" took place from late evening to early morning when the deceased was buried just before dawn or at sunrise. There used to be music, dancing, drinking, and eating at the wake keeping. It was very expensive but something in the culture. However, that kind of wake keeping no longer exists for the most part. In its place, since "everybody is now a Christian," I learnt, there is service of songs from late afternoon to early evening (4-6 pm) preceding the day of interment. Past for the most part too are the days when corpses remained in morgues for three, six, ten months, or even a year or more. The Catholic Church and some other churches demand burial within about two weeks and not too long after the death. This would save money from mortuary fees. Also the longer the postponement of the burial, the longer the preparation for the burial, the more expensive the burial is expected to be.

While there has been cost-cutting on some aspects of death-related ceremonies, more expenses must have entered other areas. Death is now a whole business with complex intersections. The family or person taking charge of the burial as of a parent (mother, father, or foster parent) has to hire undertakers, pall bearers, music bands with performers, caterers to provide food and drinks, party planners for canopies or tents, chairs and other seating arrangements, orators or emcees, and security detail of paid mobile police, army or police. It is a long list that drains the celebrant of money all the time and each according to his or her means. So there are burial ceremonies that could cost from between a half million to ten million naira or even more. For those who have the money, it is a smooth sail. For others, they have to borrow to make a grand impression and face their debts afterwards. The Urhobo people have a belief, or rather a saying, that one gets rich after burying one's father or mother. May it be so! But I also think it is a way of encouraging one to spend as much as possible. I have heard of those who incurred so much debt thinking they would have financial assistance from relatives and friends and having nothing or very little back at the end of the expensive ceremony. One of such "celebrants" died months after the father's burial. It must have been as a result of disappointment or depression or heart attack resulting from the failed expectations of wealth! For those in many societies, friends and relatives often commiserate with them with some money. But it is said that the sand one brings out digging a pit is never enough to refill it. I wonder why but get the meaning. To have a good party and be praised by everybody, my grandmother would say, shows that one is a foolish spender! It is not good to be praised by everybody.

I attended at least three burial ceremonies during the period I was in Effurun. Let me recount two of them: one at Ododegho near Ughelli, and the other at Esaba near Okwagbe. At Ododegho, it was the first cousin of my friend Dr. Jonathan who was being buried. The deceased was also the senior brother of a professor friend of mine. There had been conflicts as to where the retired military major should be buried, at Ughelli where he built a house or at Ododegho where his junior brother, the professor, built a house for him after he died. It was a tussle between the sons and the extended family, often common among the Urhobo. They even went to court over where the deceased should be buried until the case was withdrawn and my friend went from Sapele to Ododegho three times to have the conflict resolved. It was arrived at that the deceased would be buried in his birthplace of Ododegho but there would be two receptions after, one at the burial site in Ododegho and the other at the children's place in Ughelli.

Family members and friends of the deceased who have not met for a very long time tend to meet at burial ceremonies. Despite the cloak of anonymity that I thought I was wearing, I met a few people I had known while in secondary school. It was a colorful gathering with people dressed traditionally in Urhobo attire, family members in specially chosen attire, and others in simple attire. There were representatives of the military, since the person being buried was once an infantryman. Water and crackers were served on tables and fuller entertainment followed after the interment. The interment took place after the military's twenty or so gun volleys as their final salute to a departed comrade. It is difficult to keep oneself invisible in such a gathering. One of the attendees, a retired professor and former federal minister, saw me and we embraced. That public gesture might have given me out as somebody perhaps important to the *otota*, the official orator of the ceremony. It was soon announced that I was in attendance. I think what happens in these ceremonies is that the more big names of professors and chiefs the orators can throw about, the more impressive the ceremony is said to be.

The *otota*, self-styled orator, impressed me as the epitome of greed that is the common denominator of many in the land. His performance was self-centered. He did not talk about the deceased who was a military officer who fought during the Nigerian Civil War. The late major's children were themselves distinguished, I understand. Even the deceased's brother is a great professor known across the land after teaching at both Ahmadu Bello University in the North and

Delta State University in Abraka. Though retired, he was still teaching at the Niger Delta University at Amassoma in Bayelsa State. He has children, one of whom is a medical officer in Delta State University. Rather than talk about these people, the self-proclaimed orator singled out the former minister to lavish praises upon as the epitome of the caring and generous man. To my astonishment, the subject of the praise-singing came out in his traditional attire of a Victorian long-sleeved shirt, a Dutch-manufactured wrapper, a Pakistani hat, Spanish beads, and a made-in-China walking stick. That was typical of the Urhobo chief's attire. He brought out bundles of twenty-naira notes to "spray" at the orator who smiled sheepishly as he invented more outlandish metaphors and encomiums to pour at his benefactor. The scene lasted up to ten minutes with attention riveted at the orator and the ex-minister, the praise-singer and his idol. There was no doubt that both of them enjoyed the harangue.

By the time of the entertainment, about half, if not more than half, the attendees had left. No doubt to attend the deceased major's children's other reception at Ughelli. There was plenty of food to eat. I did not eat there but was given a small "cooler" that I was told had rice and meat. The celebrants here, the deceased's brother and wife, distributed gifts of plastic buckets, umbrellas, writing pads, and other articles to the remaining people. The family had "greeted" my table with some money. We were three at the table, Chief Ikpighwren, Mr. Wilson Erhirhie, and me. The chief shared the money because he was the senior. I took bottles of water because it was hot and humid. It was an outing that I enjoyed.

I also attended the burial of Professor G. G. Darah's aunt who had raised him and so he presented her as his mother. That was at Esaba. I had no idea of where Esaba was, except that it was close to Okwagbe. At the same time, some people talked about it as the end of Urhobo land before you entered Ijo land. I knew it was by a river which separated

Ughelli North Local Government from a Delta Ijo Local Government. Two roads led to Esaba—a river route you took in a boat from Aladja to the place, or a land route. I chose the land route. I had to drive to Okwagbe and pass through some rickety bridges and get there. Much as I like water and rivers, I preferred to drive a long distance rather than taking the shorter route in which I had to leave my car somewhere and be ferried by boat to Esaba. I was happy I chose the land route. I passed through towns and villages that featured great *udje* performances in the past. I saw the network of roads through Ohwahwa to Okwagbe Waterside. From Okwagbe the road there was poorly maintained but that was no problem for a 4-Runner to ply. I was impressed by the fairly pristine forest and wetlands. I could now put into perspective G. G. Darah's background and his interest in wetlands. Dark waters with brown leaves and disabled boats were by the narrow sandy roadside. It was in the dry season and I learnt there was no way of getting to Esaba with a car in the raining season when the roads were covered with water. A few farmlands stood by the roadside. The environment was cool from the waters and the forests. We passed Odebala where there was one burial ceremony too. I gave a ride to two women from Okwagbe and dropped them at the first burial ceremony and proceeded alone to Esaba.

Esaba is a small village and now has an elementary school. This was a sign of progress because G.G. Darah went to elementary school in Okwagbe several miles away and one can imagine walking that distance during the raining season. It was easy to get to the compound where the burial ceremony was taking place. I arrived early and within thirty minutes the place was filling up. There was an *udje* troupe I had contributed to bring to the occasion and it performed as the ceremony filled up. With Darah's popularity, the village was crowded despite its extreme remoteness. I enjoyed the *udje* performance and a few times the troupe had to be "sprayed" with money as custom demands at such occasions. I gave some cash to Peter to help me "spray" since I didn't want to be noticed. Again, as in the previous burial ceremony at Ododegho, the orator discovered me and chanted my name as a writer and professor. His praises did not pull me off my seat but again I sent money to him through Peter.

There is something memorable that took place there that brought out my distaste of prevailing greed and the Urhobo chieftaincy institution and its titles. There was one table set in front to serve about ten of us. Two men who said they were Urhobo chiefs from where I don't know drew the table closer to themselves and soon sat to preside over it as their inherited property. They identified one woman sitting to my left as also a chief. We had three chiefs, two professors, three lecturers, and two other people at the table. The celebrants, the family of the deceased, welcomed us with kola nuts, drinks, and cash. It looks bizarre but the burial was a celebration because the woman had lived eighty-nine years. So the family had acted as custom demands to entertain us three times with each member dropping some bills after the official family general welcome offering. Small as some gifts might be of twenty or fifty naira, with each member of the family putting onto the plate his or her own gift, it all amounted to a good sum of money. One of the male chiefs, a rather skinny man, immediately rushed to collect the money as if appointed our table's treasurer. Chief Longthroat was a gaunt-looking man, slight and light, and his shirt seemed to be too big for him. He had a voice that offended the ears with its sharpness. He was noisy as if drunk. Came time to share the money, as custom also demands before people begin to leave for home, and the self-appointed treasurer, Chief Longthroat, without announcing the total amount on the plate, started sharing the money. Nobody knew how much was there and only he knew what was there. He stood, held the many bills together and counted some notes to give the three of them that he called chiefs. In his face I saw somebody who had come to get some naira to take home. I drew his attention to the fact that we were ten on the table and not only three. He told me that the money was only for the chiefs. I asked him who said so. He said it was the tradition at ceremonies to do that.

"When we went to greet our guests here, how much did you and your so-called chiefs put down that you are taking by yourself what all of us are given?" I asked him.

"That's the way we do it?"

"How do you do it?"

"Chiefs share the money among themselves," he explained.

"Are you more important than the professors and other university teachers here or what?"

"That's the way we do it," he again said.

I saw my fellow professor and the others at the table quiet. A lady colleague eyed me in a way as if saying that I should leave the chap alone. That attitude would continue to fuel the greed of the so-called chiefs who buy their titles from greedy chieftains who call themselves kings. I gave the greedy chief one disdainful look and turned away. Three minutes later, he tried to give me sixty naira. He stretched his palm to me offering the money. I looked at him again with scorn and threw the sixty naira at him. It fell on the ground and he stooped down to pick the money. Some minutes later he left.

I was not happy with the way a female colleague explained things to me.

"Ah, that's what they do-o!" she said.

"Why should we allow that kind of greed? Why should the chiefs whose titles you can buy with as low as five thousand naira and many of whom have questionable characters be allowed to get away with such behavior?" I again asked.

"I don't know but that's the way they behave. Nobody challenges them here-o!" she explained.

I was happy I had challenged a bad habit that folks tolerated. I am not surprised that the land breeds dictators because nobody challenges even these petty chiefs who are in their behavior like thieves.

I left giving a ride to the colleague going to Okuokoko just before Effurun.

"You shouldn't have thrown the money back at him," she advised. "It is not good and somebody diabolical or violent could react and it is not worth it."

"Yes, I lost my cool because of the greed in the name of a chief," I said.

"Yes, don't be angry with these native people. It serves you no good."

"Thanks," I told her.

Reflecting on it, I knew I made a mistake to throw the money back at the man. I could have just resisted its coming to my hands or gently put it back on the plate on the table. It is one of my actions at home that I regretted. I ought to have done better than I did and I feel the others who ignored the chiefs did a better job than my angry protest.

I drove back passing another land route through much of the old kingdom of songs of Ughievwen. Towns I had heard so much about were there—Otughievwe, Iwhrekan, Edjophe, and Ekakpamre. One incident stood out on my return home. There were many army checkpoints resulting from the insecurity from armed robbers and kidnapers in the area. So as soon as I joined the Port Harcourt-Effurun Road, there were up to five lanes where there should be two on our side of the road. It is common practice for drivers to drive brainlessly as if they were animals. Those from one side tended to close the opposite lane as if it is also theirs to ply. Once the right lane was moving slowly, they created many more lanes and eventually clogged the road to a standstill. I was pushed from the right lane I was following outside to the curb and had to stay there imploring with signs other drivers to give me way to enter the main road. It took over twenty minutes before someone held back for me to enter the right lane. It took another thirty minutes to cross the Ekrerhavwen checkpoint. From there it was easy drive to Warri after dropping the woman at Okuokoko.

Weddings take place every week in Nigeria. It is one of those events where families show not just their solidarity by coming together but also spending as much money as available to boost their egos. Marriage is one event that brings family members to rejoice at one of them taking a partner to procreate and extend the family name. Everybody is expected to marry and young men and women have it as a major goal to have a partner. For men, it is much easier but not as easy for women. It becomes an embarrassment when a young woman does not get a suitor or husband. By the time she is "over-ripe," as some are described, she becomes an embarrassment to the family. It is a society that is not tolerant of single women or men. In fact, women feel that being married adds status to them; hence some who are doctors or professors go as far as to proclaim themselves as Professor (Mrs) Iammarried or Dr. (Mrs.) Iamnotaspinster! Of course, one asks, why are there no Professor (Mr.) Iammarried or Dr. (Mr.) Iamnotabachelor? But that is how women perpetuate their own subordination in the patriarchal society that abuses and disrespects them.
I have heard of weddings of Nigerians in foreign countries. The elites, the rich, now leave Nigeria and fly hundreds of guests in special plane charters to foreign countries for weddings in Dubai, Cyprus, Malaysia, and Ghana. My sister-in-law attended one of such weddings in which the father of the bride lavished hundreds of millions of naira to sponsor the wedding. Nobody knows where Nigerians will go next to display their ill-gotten wealth in wedding ceremonies. I will not be surprised if a family bought space in the Russian international space station for his daughter or son and the

invited guests to create another record. I believe if that were done, the next family would aim at Mars or even heaven for the ceremony!

I attended both the traditional and the church weddings of a niece-in-law in Warri in February of 2014. Usually the church asks the traditional bride-price paying ceremony, called traditional wedding, to take place before the church wedding. One of the new ways is to have the traditional and the church weddings to take place on the same date to cut down on expenditures. Weddings had become expensive because of so many things to take care of. Earlier the introduction to the family which was done by the future bridegroom and two or three trusted family members visiting the bride-to-be's parents and a few family members had ballooned to become a gathering of many representatives on both sides. In fact, some celebrants bring musicians and make a big party of the introduction. Before I left Nigeria in 1989, there was no introduction as of this magnitude but our people had copied the new practice from the Yoruba who are known for throwing lavish big parties.

The traditional bride-price paying ceremony was done in the father's sitting room in Notoma Street, Essi Layout, in Warri. Those who attended were directly from the two families, unlike the church wedding which had a multitude of family, friends, and well-wishers of both bride and groom. Five priests officiated at the wedding Mass. The reception took place in the father's compound in Notoma Street. This was a modest ceremony meant to cut costs. Others who have the means and want to show off would rent a hall in a big hotel or a place at the PTI Staff Club for the reception. It appeared in this one that the bride's family prepared the foods served. I praise the father of the bride for standing firm in doing the reception in his compound and in a modest manner rather than showing off and later regretting the needless expenditures.

Professor Toyin Falola's installation as the Bobabitan of Ibadan was a great ceremony. I had just returned from a conference of the African Literature Association in Johannesburg on April 16 to Effurun. I arrived a day earlier, on April 18. I was picked from the Eagle station near the University of Ibadan directly to attend an introduction ceremony. One of Toyin's male relations was being introduced to the future family-in-law. It is known all over Nigeria that the Yoruba like big parties and this was a very grand one for just an introduction. You can imagine what the real wedding would be. It was held in a grand hall that was well adorned. The entertainment and music would almost dwarf many of the wedding receptions in the Warri area.

The following morning at about nine, we set out for the Olubadan's Palace in Ibadan. It was a ceremony of dignified guests ranging from many of us from the Diaspora and family and friends of the eminent professor within Nigeria. I have to praise the Olubadan's Traditional Council for selecting their illustrious son abroad for such an honor. In comparison with Yoruba traditional rulers, I felt Urhobo ovies did not seem to care about their intellectuals. The same Olubadan's traditional council had also honored Wole Soyinka the same week. There was music and a traditional orator who seems self-appointed who talked and made people laugh. However, he seemed to have overstepped his bounds when he started to demand money from the guests. Since the hall was small, only a few close guests of the celebrants went in while a television screen set up outside displayed the entire ceremony inside. The Oba was very old, as is traditional of Ibadan, since the oldest chief assumes the throne. Some senior chiefs acted for him. The peak of the ceremony came with the Olubadan presenting Toyin and his wife and dressing both of them with similar handcrafted caps with some fresh leaves attached to each to symbolize the evergreen memory expected of the Bobabitan and his wife. As a historian and creative writer of poetry and memoirs, Toyin's title is very appropriate as he is the chronicler of Ibadan history. In fact, he has written a seminal work on Ibadan history and done a memoir on the Agbekoya Uprising of the 1960s in the Yoruba area. After the inner palace ceremony, the newly installed chiefs strolled out and we took photographs before heading for the reception in another part of Ibadan.

The reception was majestic and meets one's expectation of a big Yoruba party. There were drummers and singers. In attendance were some of the most distinguished Yoruba, albeit Nigerian, intellectuals. I could see that intellectuals among the Yoruba people are highly respected and recognized. The vast hall was well decorated and there was plenty of food and drinks for all. There was dancing. It was colorful for the *aso ebi*, *aso oke*, and other majestic dresses worn. We posed for photos, and the installation of Bobabitan of Ibadan is one of the most heart-warming ceremonies I attended in Nigeria during my one year stay.

*   *   *

No doubt, Nigerians know how to follow other people's ways even when they don't care about theirs. Many Nigerians phoned me while I was in Nigeria congratulating me on July 4 with "Happy Independence Day!" Shamefully on October 1, Nigeria's Independence Day, I heard of no greetings. The press, social media, and many individuals publicized Halloween, the last day of October. And a few children of the elites and rich in Lagos and Abuja ludicrously dressed in Halloween costumes. I did not hear any pastor condemn the action of the Nigerian kids in scary uniform and trick-a-treating as Satanic.

Globalization has fully claimed many Nigerians into its trail. While in Nigeria, I did not hear of Thanksgiving. Of course, in touch with my family, I knew the United States was agog with Thanksgiving preparations. I normally did not see that day as necessary as my people and I thanked God every day. I normally separated myself from those waging war against turkeys and ate fish that day. I had other reservations about that day which has to do with seizing other people's land and thanking God for it, if that's what the thanksgiving is about. But I was in Nigeria. Nigerians knew about Black Friday and Cyber Monday and with credit cards and online sales, they would plunge into the busy networks to place orders for their desires.

Valentine's Day was the most popular. Europe and America do things and Nigerians follow. February 14 is a popular day in Nigeria. At the PTI Club that evening, it was a mammoth crowd that would fill a huge football stadium. Pairs of lovers drove in or were dropped by taxis to have an evening of barbecued fresh fish and drinks to celebrate their love relationships. I later heard that the accommodation part of the complex was fully booked for lovers in Effurun and Warri and the environs to really make Valentine's Day a sexy one.

11

ABUJA

Abuja looks very impressive for a visitor, Nigerian or foreign. Driving into Abuja from the Nnamdi Azikiwe International Airport or coming from the South through Abaji or from the North through Zuba or Keffi, one has the feeling that the well-paved roads are leading to a beautiful city. There is a maze of groomed roadwork with bridges here and there. One is not disappointed entering Abuja. Even the outskirts of town promise a beautiful and planned city. If the roads into the city could be so beautiful, if the outskirts of town could boast of so many beautiful housing developments, the city itself must be superb. One is not disappointed on this account.

Abuja compares well with many well-planned world capitals. After all, it was built with a big chunk of oil money to be the federal capital; a befitting capital of an oil-producing country. It was built the same way Dodoma was conceived to be the administrative capital of Tanzania, Brasilia for Brazil, and Putra Jaya for Malaysia. It was meant to be far away from the madding crowd of Lagos. Federal legislators and the Presidency would have a quiet non-commercial place to reflect on policies and steer the nation aright. It is set in the open savannah and part of the city built on rocks. In fact, the Presidential Villa sits on a rock and is aptly called Aso Rock. It is a city that is exposed to the elements; there are no forests, and it takes the full brunt of the harmattan during the cold season. Dust haze is a constant feature of the atmosphere during the harmattan. It tested the ability of landscapers. It made landscapers and city maintainers to have lawns and flowers that would make the landscape look more European or foreign than African.

But it is a city also meant to be central to Nigeria so that all the cardinal points could meet there. It is a compromise of a family quarrelling over where to place their common property. And so from all directions Abuja stands at the center to please northerners and southerners that they have a new capital that is central and not too much to the south and not too much to the north. Whatever the geographical location, Abuja politically is not southern like Lagos but northern. But still it is an acceptable south-of-north position that settled a family feud.

Abuja is divided into Areas numbered in a weird manner as if the authority numbering them has problems with memory, often skipping some numbers for others. So, while the city was planned, the naming sometimes betrays lack of planning. I saw Areas 1, 2, 3, 8, and 11. Maybe all the Areas have not been completed but there is no room to have the other unused figures. Abuja also has districts. For instance, there is Wuse I and there is also Wuse II as if the town-planners and administrators lacked more names. Maitama, Garki, and Central Districts are some of the most cosmopolitan parts of the city with skyscrapers, shopping centers, and an array of urban features.

Compared to most Nigerian towns that are not planned, there is always a sense of direction as one drives or moves in Abuja. There is almost a ring road circling the city and one only needs to have a sense of where one is going not to be lost. The GPS in my friend's 4-Runner functions well. I am amazed because I can't imagine GPS working well in Lagos. I can say that an experienced driver will always find his or her way in Abuja once one knows the contours of the city. But things are changing so fast in development because of new accommodations for the people flocking into the city that new housing areas are getting lost in the original grid of the city.

Things are also changing because of plots of land that each ruling government gives out or sells that will be bound to choke the city traffic-wise in a matter of several years. While El Rufai, the former Federal Capital Territory Minister, I learnt, had enforced vigorously the territory's plan by demolishing houses of even big men, politicians and military officers, the situation has not been the same in subsequent administrations. It is like looking at a beautiful woman that one knows that age is bound to ravage into a lesser beauty with time. The signs are already there for Abuja to deteriorate but let me testify to what I see now.

Abuja is one of the most expensive cities or capitals in the world, I came to understand while there. My experience confirms this. Hotels are expensive compared to Washington, DC, London, Kuala Lumpur, and many other capitals. Most three-star or four-star hotels charge more than 30,000 naira per night. That is the equivalent of $200 which is pretty high and could fetch you more in developed countries. But there is no gain-saying it that Abuja has a multiplicity of hotels. Few hotels belong to any chain. Transcorp was once owned by Hilton. There is Sheraton. There are at least two functioning Chelsea Hotels. Of the private-owned, there are many. I stayed at the Vine in Area 1 for two nights at 30,000 naira per night. I was in the Rockview Hotel in Wuse II for several weeks and that was about 38,000 naira a night for a room. These are just moderate ones, with many of the others too steep for me.

I believe the expensive nature of Abuja hotels could be because of the affluent legislators who live there or who put in their guests for free. I had a feeling that many of the young women who were in Rockview and 3J's did not appear to me to have the money to lodge there but paid for. I watched a scene at Rockview Royale where a rich politician brought about ten young women for a buffet dinner of 4,000 naira plus wines and hard liquor of all sorts. Another reason for the steep prices is that state and federal government officials and workers in companies and parastatals do not stay in hotels with their own monies but get their bills settled by their institutions. And international visitors are in Abuja for one reason or the other and are prepared to pay from their state or company's purses.

Rented accommodation is very expensive in Abuja. Buying a home is beyond even the middle class's reach, unless the person has other ways of making money. Those in business can do that. A simple three-bedroom could cost as much as thirty million naira and that is a good buy! Bigger and more sophisticated duplexes would cost over sixty million. But there is so much disparity in Abuja that where you have ten folks squeezing themselves into a room, one person can buy a big house for a hundred million naira. And that will be done not by a mortgage arrangement of thirty years or so, as I am used to in the United States, but paid for in cash! There are so many rich people in Nigeria and many live in Abuja. My friend Ola was able to get a three bedroom for four million naira a year. I was staying for five to ten months since I was meant to teach at the University of Abuja for half my fellowship and do research in the Delta for the other half. An unfurnished room, a single room called sleep-in or some other name was to cost me 960,000 naira a year in the Jabi Lake area. So much money for an unfurnished room! I could not pay that out of what I had and buy furniture I would abandon after five months or at most ten months of stay.

It is in Abuja that you find legislators, especially the older ones, who are like snakes casting off their skins in each political incarnation, have big houses in the city and get the government to pay them to live in their own houses got through government patronage. There are areas where only political figures have huge houses. A cab driver showed me what he said were houses of the big men in the House and Senate. Their official quarters were furnished with money they vote for themselves.

One observation of Abuja before I talk about other aspects of the city is the naming of streets. Current serving politicians, government officials, and military officers have roads and streets named after them. I don't need to call the names but there those names strike you as too self-serving. Why not name streets and roads to honor the dead? Only a few names deserve to be there. My only problem, after visiting other countries, is that there is no street named after an artist or writer! Even discredited politicians or leaders have streets named after them. The politicians don't have any sense of humility not to name streets after themselves. It is a shame that Wole Soyinka who won the Nobel Prize for Literature has no street named after him. Nor Chinua Achebe who exposed Nigeria's name to the world in his novels that have been translated to over thirty languages! The Nigerian authorities do not have any regard for writers and other artists. They only care about those in power, military and civilian politicians.

Abuja is a commuter city. Very few can afford to live in the city. A city planned for only government civil servants has more than doubled its population in only two decades and the traffic is already getting as bad as the old capital of Lagos that was abandoned for a central and more relaxed city. Workers, I mean drivers, traders, and the lower class flow from Mararaba and Nyanya through the gauntlet of a pass into town in the morning traffic ordeal. After the bomb blast in Nyanya it took over three hours to pass through the Camel's Needle of less than five miles—the road ferrying commuters to the belly of the beast. Houses in Mararaba and Nyanya exhibit the socio-economic inequalities in Nigeria. Much of Mararaba is made up of slums, especially Across the Bend and other areas two blocks from the Abuja-Keffi Road. From the northwest are Kubwa and Zuba ferrying another mass into Abuja. And from other areas from the South as far down as Gwagwalada, Giri, and nearer and more upbeat housing developments to the capital city.

Abuja is many cities in one despite everything said. Within what could be described as Abuja are new developments: Gwarimpa, Jabi, Sun City, Lugbe, Mechanic

Village, Garden City, and so many others. The architecture is modern but each new housing development tends to have a uniform architectural style, including roofing. Abuja roads are fine; all done by Julius Berger known to have the best expertise and experience in road-making in the country. For some good reasons, either the Federal Ministry of Works or the Federal Capital Territory has never flinched on giving the roads to a credible builder. Construction is always going on and a maze of roads is trying to accommodate the ever-increasing number of cars and commuters flooding the city. Light rail lines are being constructed but I knew the light rail would not start working when I was there. Many Nigerian rail projects had been constructed with billions of dollars and then abandoned like the Ajaokuta-Aladja rail network. I hope the light rail in Abuja would not suffer the same fate of abandonment. For one thing, things work in Abuja because the Federal Government, despite many incompetent actions, wants to be seen as doing well. On roads I give them a high grade for sticking to a good road maker rather than party-owned companies that win contracts of roads in other parts of the country and are bogged down by demand for more money for work not done.

But roads may be smooth as in Abuja and still be so accident prone. A city with intermittent light supply cannot run an efficient traffic system. Light is not the sole problem of Abuja roads. The intersections in Abuja are some of the worst one can find in a city of that size and importance. There are intersections where one is not sure of who has right of way—for example, where Ahmadu Bello and Ibrahim Babangida intersect in Wuse II. There are so many of them. There are no lights or robots at intersections to control traffic and when it is raining or dark, God help those who venture out in the streets of Abuja. One is more likely to die of a road accident in Abuja than anything else, including kidnaping, shooting, or armed robbery, I learnt from some foreign experts in town during my orientation week.

Abuja is a clinical town. It has no roots. There is no traditional ruler as in Lagos, the federal capital that was abandoned. The ethnic group that owns the land, the Gwari, has little or no stake in the city. Since they are scattered into Kogi, Kaduna, Nassarawa, and the Federal Capital Territory, they are a minority in every state and so do not have the numbers to fight for a cause. There may not be many highly educated ones to mobilize their people to assert their political will. And so the Federal Government took over the land of the FCT from different states that the Gwari occupy as its own. The lack of history and culture in Abuja makes it not a place to visit unless one has a political or business matter to attend to. It amazes me that while Abuja is an administrative place and there are few industries, contractors and many people from different parts of the country continue to flock there for "business." That is because the national cake is shared there, and who is near or there takes a bigger slice! The legislators exercise power in Abuja. Lobbying is a profession in Abuja. Money is disbursed from Abuja for federal projects across the country and so Abuja is both centrifugal and centripetal in Nigerian politics and business.

Abuja may have mowed lawns and flowers, but lacks what attracts people to a city. There are no statues of heroes and no iconic places. There are small parks but many are being taken away for some other uses than what they were originally planned for. As noted earlier, Jabi Lake Park was said to have been sold to private hands to use commercially as an entertainment center. I will not be surprised that in another five to ten years the new owner would turn the park into a housing estate and build new houses for the increasing number of influx into town. It is not too late to make Abuja a really national capital city by having statues of national heroes there. It is not too late to create zoos or museums there to attract visitors and tourists and to give people in town somewhere to go on weekends and public holidays. It is not too late to have a big park that will attract folks to relax daily when they are free or at weekends. Currently, Abuja is more than half empty on weekends and on major holidays like Christmas and New Year the city's population is reduced to less than a third.

There is social and night life in Abuja as will not be found in many other places in Nigeria. There are the likes of Central City Park where you can go for grilled or roasted fish or meat. The ambience is beautiful. There are so many areas like that all over town. At the Roses, near Crystal Palace Hotel, you can have the best of *isi-ewu* with live bands playing on weekends. In addition to Transcorp, Sheraton, Rockview, Chelsea, and many other three-to-five star hotels, one can have a great social life in Abuja, if one has the money. I can say with money Abuja is a sweet place to experience.

Abuja attracts young men and women searching for jobs. The prospects are not good for those who don't have godfathers and godmothers. Many of the boys end up doing menial jobs. The situation is trickier for girls because of their gender. Some may end up being girlfriends or mistresses of the political elite. A few are lucky to find work but may still get attached to the men, a majority of whom are married but left their wives at home in their respective states. I met a young lady who worked in a hotel. Her work ranged from the reception desk attendant to taking care of the bar. She told me she was working to save money to go to school because she had already had her Senior Secondary School Certificate. I much doubt that she would not be distracted from her education because of the lecherous men who were likely to "toast" her. Paid about 12,000 naira a month, I knew it was impossible for anybody to survive on 12,000 in Abuja. She refused to tell me where she lived but I guessed far away in one of those suburbs, unless she lived with somebody else. I knew another lady in a drinking spot in Wuse II. She worked from about 4 o'clock till past midnight when she left there for where she lived in Nyanya, and got home sometimes by 4 a.m. She was a pretty lady and I asked her why she chose to do that job in which she was not well paid but relied on tips. Again, she came to Abuja to make it. That statement was pregnant with meaning. For those girls that catch the sugar daddies and the young men who catch sugar mommies, their tale of Abuja would be different. Most of the legislators are mugus that the young women treat for hefty sums. I had been in a Sienna minivan traveling from Warri to Abuja and listened intently as three young ladies talked about their Abuja exploits which were very lucrative. They boasted of not just having several millions in their bank accounts but traveled overseas at their mugus' expense.

I see Abuja as beautiful. But it is too clinical, too much unlike the rest of Nigeria. It is a window-dressed capital for the rest of the world to see us for what we are not. It is very well dressed but sterile. It has no fragrances as of goats, sheep, cows, chickens, and others as in other towns or in the outskirts as I saw in satellite villages of Aku and Apo. Abuja is like a human being without human odor but just there. Yes, there is social life at night but it remains that type of enigmatic beauty that taunts one but drains one—if not physically, financially!

There are many invisible things about Abuja, I am told by a friend. I could be there for one year, three years, or more but would not be able to observe or see so much happening. There is so much beyond the pale of the eyes. Abuja is not only the federal capital city but also the capital city of medicine-men, babalawos, dibias, healers, and marabouts. So strong is the temptation to win political elections, retain seats, get political appointments, and make money, at all cost that the people we see during the day often go at night to consult babalawos for strong medicines to enhance their positions. I am told during the day and on Fridays and Sundays many will go to mosques and churches respectively but many of the same people at night patronize the medicine men that congregate in Abuja's suburbs from all parts of the country. There is even an international ring from Sudan and Mali and other places there to be consulted for mystical powers to be strong politically and make a hell of money. Many of them, I am told by the person who says that I am blind if I see only roads and hotels in Abuja, now charge in foreign currencies and attend to only those who can afford dollars, euros, and pounds. It is not surprising that the Nigerian rich would think that paying with foreign exchange would enhance the efficacy of medicines made for him. As they say in Warri, as it comes it goes. Since the legislators make easy money, they have to spend it too easily. And that is upon demands for cows or human beings to be buried alive. I understand one marabout asked for a 25-litre jerry can of human blood to make somebody remain in his political seat for life! I can't tell whether that was accomplished or can ever be accomplished.

My lasting impression of the Federal Capital is a poem I had to write.

The New Lotus Eaters
(after a three-week stay in Abuja)

They leave home lean of body after selling all they have
of material and soul to win the people's mandate to rob;

they arrive in Abuja or any of the satellite capital cities
refuged in lavish rooms a world away from tribal shacks.

Once there they scramble for spread-out lotus dishes,
and they lounge in halls and guesthouses of sloth—

they forget what they were sent there for, to fight battles
that will give dignity to their people as human beings;

the representatives forget they are messengers of hope
to bring succor to desperate folks languishing in despair;

they eat the flowering food, fall into delirium that drives
them to further consume the entire share of their senders.

They hide in their paunches the billions meant for roads
and bridges that will take desperate people out of misery;

obese from the cult of theft they are sworn to by Speakers,
they waddle in sloth and wander no more to seek a cure

for folks at home being strangled by multiple afflictions;
they no longer remember the message they came with

because they live in the land of lotus eaters, capital city;
brains anomied from the deliciously intoxicating wine

they share constantly as their dividend of democracy;
night and day they distill wine from lotus to consume.

They invite marabouts and other fetish priests to their dens
to save them from being lynched by demons of their lust;

they know not that the thief will never enjoy peace or safety—
he will forever be hounded by enraged spirits of stolen wealth!

Most incapacitated die where they had been sent to fight;
they are already dead and buried in infamy in new homes;

others possessed by the diabolic aroma of the lotus
and the loot they frolic in die like their kind, vultures.

Once arrived at the capital or headquarters, the scramble
of human-costumed animals begins for the lotus intoxicant;

they transform without effort into goats, pigs, sheep, cows,
pythons, and other beasts stampeding in the oil-glutted soil

for what only non-humans care for as the meaning of life;
they are practically animals without human minds and souls.

Surely, there's no island here to grow abundance of lotus
but thanks to oil, the land's awash with the hallucinating plant

& in his wandering the minstrel watches the population
and swears not to make the city of lotus-eaters his home.

12

MAMA TOKO'S MODEL ORPHANAGE

(In a moment of introspection, I wrote this short story.)

Nomate Toko was not only a figure with national name recognition but also one highly connected to different kinds of powerful people. She knew political leaders at federal and state levels. She knew businessmen and women, she knew religious leaders and who was who in the entire country. She looked dignified and graceful in her early fifties. She had an affable personality that made her stand out in any circle in which she found herself. No one was therefore surprised when she was awarded the Grand Order of the Niger, the highest national award in the land. To many Nigerians, she deserved the award more than most of the others who were also conferred with the honor—politicians, party henchmen and women, contractors, businessmen, professor speech writers, and others that everybody knew were self-centered, sycophantic, and corrupt. The list of the recipients of the annual honors had till now become a national joke to the extent that disgraced politicians, robbers-turned-chiefs, and worse personalities had been conferred with the highest national award.

Comedians had poked fun at the recipients of recent national honors whom they described as pen robbers, chiefly thieves, and juvenile adults. The public always wondered how names of corrupt, indicted, and convicted governors and other politicians got to be slipped into the list and given such awards that should be sacred. They believed no Selection Committee worth its name would include convicts and other scandalous men and women as national role models. To them, honoring such dishonorable people was like honoring vultures and hyenas. Many other recipients literally bought the honors with campaign contributions or paid bribes to administrators of the award. Among those who got national recognition were unknown folks whose wealth's source nobody knew. Many cynics believed that dogs of the powerful and vultures would soon be on that list.

Nobody believed, with the name she had made, that Nomate Toko's award was tied to a payback or a kind of quid pro quo; unlike those of most other awardees. Nobody believed her award was lobbied for as was done for many others. In the country, the good people were rarely recognized or honored; they were more often than not always passed over for mediocre ones. For a change a good woman, many people felt, a selfless woman, a sensitive person, and one who really cared for the disadvantaged had been nominated and given a great award. That was how things should be, people believed. Even before the presentation of the award, she received so many congratulatory messages from well-wishers on radio, television, and newspapers. The *Concord* and the *Guard*, in particular, had almost a whole week with pages bought to pay tribute to Nomate Toko.

In a country of so much hoopla with ethnicities, nobody ever cared where Mama Toko, as she was popularly called, came from. She had no marks to identify her. Nor did she have any accent that interfered with her English to betray her tribal origin. She wore what could be described as national dresses. She was a polyglot and spoke each of the nine languages she was fluent at as a native speaker. She was indeed a tribe-less person. Every ethnic group would have liked to claim her because of the good work she was believed to be doing. She was a new type of Mother Theresa, who was not a Catholic sister but a missionary at home. It was good that she did not emigrate to either the First World or some other part of the Third World as many missionaries in the country were then doing.

She was of average height and size. Her physique belied the now legendary fame that often preceded her before those who knew her in person. Did they expect an Amazon woman, muscular and gigantic who could throw any man down? Or did they expect Mrs. Fumilayo Ransom-Kuti spitting fire to threaten men to abandon their patriarchal privileges and cede human rights to women? Could she be one of those Aba women who rose against armed British colonialists and forced them to rescind obnoxious "head tax" impositions? Nobody preceded her name with any prefix. She might be married, divorced, widowed, or never married, but who cared about that when it came to Mama Toko? She was tender, feminine, but not one that men would call pretty. But she was enamored to all the big men, and to big women too for that matter. She exuded a certain mystique and those mystified by her personality wondered how she came to be so beloved by everybody in a country of so many women-haters. No man or gossip columnist had used the p word to describe her in a country where so many, in their patriarchal arrogance and chauvinistic attitude, believed a woman could not be anything except by being a prostitute or a man's mistress. And beloved to so many she really was. She ran the best-known orphanage in the country.

Her orphanage was unique. Sanoma Children's Home had its sprawling but manicured compound in the Jabi area of Abuja. The compound was fenced round with a high wall painted white. It had an adamantine gate that glittered night and day with the bold name of the orphanage flashing as a disco club's inside lights. The gatemen were uniformed white and were always alert to those coming in or going out, saluting the drivers. They never accepted any tip, as other gatemen manning such impressive gates did.

Others ran ramshackle orphanages; Mama Toko's was a model home of neat boys and girls. The children looked well-fed and they always dressed in their starched uniforms of white at school and brown checkered in the hostels. They looked like children of the rich—their teeth shone white, their skin smooth from being fed with eggs, chicken, salmon, Irish potatoes, and other foods available at big men's tables. The gossip or rumor was that physicians, dentists, eye doctors, and other medical personnel volunteered their services free to visit the orphanage once in a while to examine the children. Every child there appeared to be enjoying supreme health. There were rumors too that only big people were allowed to adopt these children. No wonder children of the poor, who saw these children on television, were envious of these privileged orphans; they even wished their mothers and fathers dead to be orphans and be taken into Sanoma Children's Home.

Once the children's home gained national attention, newspapers, radio and television stations carried the events taking place there free. They had their Christmas Carols and Cultural Event Day to which selected members of the public were invited. You had to carry a special on Mama Toko's orphanage to show that you were supporting something good in the country. The orphanage ran kindergarten and elementary schools that paraded on television neatly uniformed boys and girls. A few were bused to a private junior high school in town.

Mama Toko, according to her workers, only considered the applications of those who were really well-off for the adoption of any of the children in Sanoma Children's Home. To these workers, the orphanage was a revolving door that transferred and transformed derelict children to good health and then to homes of middle-class or high-class men and women. Grown-up boys and girls were placed by Mama Toko in homes of rich families but it was extremely rare to see any of them years later after they left the home. But this was not a school to have an alumni association to meet years after for a reunion. If anyone expected that sort of reunion, it might not happen.

Everything seemed normal and routine in Sanoma Children's Home until a female worker took a liking for one of the girls. The woman would follow the trail of this girl and discover what none of the workers had known about where they worked. She saw the visit of a Governor who came incognito and after which the girl disappeared. When she asked for who adopted her, she was told it was not her business.

"She's in good hands," was all Mama Toko could tell Mabel.

"We thank God," she replied.

What else could she ask Mama Toko? Could she drag the truth or any secrets from her mouth? Two days later, Mama Toko was driving a new Toyota Land Cruiser that was given to her by the same Governor. She had acknowledged the gift before her workers, speaking of the Governor as one of the most generous supporters of Sanoma Children's Home. Mabel soon realized that there was so much going on unseen by the workers and the rest of the country in the affairs of Sanoma Children's Home.

The way only Mama Toko ran the home was a classic example of micro management style. Only she knew who adopted the children. Only she signed the papers and yet there were no other records filed for future reference should there be either a complaint or any effort to track the source of any specific child. Only she knew the whereabouts of the adopted children. Only Mama Toko knew what was happening in the dark. Only she knew what was in the shadows of the orphanage. After all, she was the chief executive of Sanoma Children's Home. She was not the CEO of an organization with shareholders to whom she owed any annual report. The buck ended with her, as she saw her role as proprietor and executive officer of the orphanage she had single-handedly founded and was growing.

Mama Toko's three-story duplex bungalow was impressive. Her bedroom was on the third story. She received her dignitaries on the second floor, many of whom chose to visit at odd times, especially at late night. Nobody suspected her of being loose and flirting with a stream of men. After all, female dignitaries also visited her. Her workers had access only to the first floor of the house. A woman of so much standing had no permanent housekeepers, cooks, or servants. She lived alone but seemed to be comfortable with her style of living without a permanent help. The children's home's cleaners cleaned her house during the morning hours as they cleaned the hostels of the orphans. The workers believed Mama Toko prepared her own food.

Mabel had been intrigued by the adoption of Little Meg, as she called the now alumna of Sanoma Children's Home. She had brought her to Mama Toko in the late evening after a call from her boss to that effect. On their way to Madam Toko, Little Meg cried all the way. The young girl muttered amidst sobs that she did not want to leave the home; she did not want to die because she believed that she would certainly die when taken out for adoption. Mabel was shocked because she had thought that the expectation of adoption by a rich family would make the little girl excited and happy.

"Stop that nonsense!" Mabel had shouted at her.

"No, they will kill me," the little girl persisted with a stream of copious tears flowing down her cheeks.

Neither Mama Toko nor Mabel knew how haunted with thoughts of death Little Meg had been. She had first heard the lore passed down from bigger children to younger ones that went the round in the orphanage. Did she not hear about the boy—they never called him any specific name— who had returned from being placed with a very rich man who came back briefly before being taken away again? The boy, according to the story, had been placed with a very rich man who took him to a medicine man who refused to use him for

169

whatever medicine the very rich man had wanted. According to the story, the medicine man said the spirit of the boy would not help the medicine to work and so he should be freed and taken back. The very rich man whom the boy could not identify beat him mercilessly for losing so much money on his account—the amount never told—and placed him at an intersection close to Sanoma Children's Home. Little Meg heard the boy later wandered into the orphanage and within a short time of being around and telling his experiences to a few who gathered round him was summoned by Mama Toko and taken away. Many children who had heard the story believed he must be dead. However, his story was passed from one year to another. Little Meg had nightmares in which she experienced what the boy was supposed to be used for. "What if my spirit does not refuse to be used as that boy's?" she had continued to ask herself.

In one of her nightmares, she was taken to the top of a rocky mountain and sacrificed like a goat before a big man who used her blood to bathe his body. After then the big man descended the mountain and as he descended the rock she shouted in her sleep and woke. Since then she had had the fear that she would soon be taken away ostensibly for adoption but really to be used as a sacrifice for the efficacy of a big man's money-doubling or political survival medicine.
Little Meg did not bring her things and was asked to go and bring them in another twenty minutes and return to Mama Toko's house. Mabel had chosen to give an excuse so as to have the opportunity to follow the little girl. The woman had a rare chance to ask Little Meg about what bothered her.

"How do you know the man adopting you will kill you?"

"We know that those taken out get killed," the girl said.

"How can those big men or women in cars kill the children they adopt?"

"No, they don't come to adopt. They come to buy us and use us for medicines," the little girl explained.

Mabel was shocked about the secret knowledge of children that they, adult workers in the orphanage, were not privileged to know about. She started to collect the girl's few clothes but within several minutes, Mama Toko came in as one who had come in a hurry. It appeared she had to come herself to ensure that Little Meg got back to her quickly without delay. Mama Toko badged into both Mabel and the little girl. There was no chance for Mabel to probe the girl with further questions. She knew Mama Toko expected her to leave, and she had to abandon the little girl to her fate.

Mabel who doubled as a messenger and teacher was intrigued but felt helpless. She had heard before and dismissed the rumor that the children were not really going to these so-called big men and women. All of a sudden she started to reel the film of history from the time she had spent there. Most workers did not stay more than a year or two in the orphanage; they were either dismissed or asked to go with a huge sum to start some profitable businesses. No single worker thus knew the history of the place beyond one or two years. This unusual high turnover of keepers and teachers mystified Mabel since there was a very high unemployment rate in the country.

As Mabel thought of the young girl crying hysterically, her mind flashed to things she had taken for normal. She now asked herself many questions. "Why was it that the strangest of the children or handicapped among them were the first to be adopted? The albinos, hunchbacks, blind, and cripples went faster for adoption than the rest of the orphan population. They were adopted at such speed that the more healthy and normal-looking children were at first jealous until they started to have a weird cold feeling towards the manner their physically challenged mates disappeared from their daily lives. To the outside world, Nomate Toko did not discriminate in her home—it was open to any type of orphaned children in the country that there was room for in her home. And the knowledge that she did not discriminate on whom to take in and later place in big or rich families endeared her so much to those who knew about the orphanage.

Despite the so many numbers of orphans coming in weekly and perhaps daily, adoptions were going on at the same high rate that left the place with a rather balanced population. Mabel now thought of rumors or gossips that she had heard and dismissed. Once an elderly big man came in a walking stick dressed in simple kaftan. The dress did not seem to fit him or he walked as he was not used to walking and the dress was not like what he was used to wearing. Gossip had had it from the children who had better instincts and keener eyes than their teachers that he was the President of the Federation—he walked with the same long and brushy gait as of the person they saw on television as the president. None of the teachers or children could talk publicly about the visit of the disguised big man that none could confirm with certainty.

Other instances of men and women in disguise visiting their compound came to Mabel's mind. Obas, governors, army commanders, and renowned pastors and bishops had come as ordinary big men but the children had contradicted their caregivers that these seemingly ordinary visitors were not what they were seen to be; they were very important people. When you had children from all over the country in a sort of national orphanage as Sanoma Children's Home was, now and then a child would know someone important from a place others did not know. The collective memory of the children was able to identify the different visitors no matter where they came from. However, the caregiving staff had thought the children were suffering from delusion or some other forms of mental retardation and dismissed their talks as nonsense.

*   *   *

Mabel had the hunch that soon she might be given a lump sum to retire to set up her own business or kicked out outright. She knew she had known too much for a worker in the orphanage and Mama Toko, with prescience for the littlest thing that happened around, might already know the weight of knowledge she was carrying. She continued to be haunted by the spirit of Little Meg she now believed, from her appearance to her in dreams, was not adopted by anybody but most likely used as a human sacrifice by the Governor asked by a medicine-man to produce a human, preferably a virgin girl, for a potent sacrifice that would facilitate, if not assure, his second term in office.

Awake at two in the morning, Mabel's mind opened up so many things that could be happening under her eyes without her seeing them. So much water was passing under the bridge, as she saw the situation. If she looked sharply, there was much to piece together in the seemingly efficient daily routine in the orphanage. There were things more than the prayers at dawn or before going to bed, the regular sumptuous meals, the classes, and playtime for the children. There was another narrative that was subsumed in the main daily lives of the children. Now she had amassed a memory-filled cache that all of a sudden was clear to her since her employment in Sanoma Children's Home.

Their orphanage was a breeding ground for children for all sorts of odd rituals that the big men and women of the society indulged in for political positions or money. The medicine men and women knew the big ones would not consider their medicines potent or efficacious enough without their demanding young ones, especially the most physically challenged and virgins, to prepare the medicines. And so they prescribed that their consultants bring them the ultimate animal for sacrifice that they knew was a human being. It was a delicate thing. No big man or woman, political, religious, or business, would entrust the procurement of a young boy or girl into even a confidant's hands. They wanted to keep everything to their chests. Not even their security details should be made aware of this deed because such could expose them when they fell out in future. And that was why they cultivated friendship with Nomate Toko to get the sacrificial humans from her own hands and taken directly to the attending medicine men.

Mabel in that deep night had a flash that exposed clearly why her "we-hail-thee" country was in such a mess. Even governors in difficult court cases and the President seeking masculine prowess were involved. Pastors and bishops who wanted bigger congregations and lavish offerings came for their human supplies. Wealthy folks, who wanted to more than double their already staggering amounts of money and be mentioned in Forbes among the richest in the continent, if not the entire world, also came.

The unionized medicine men and healers of the Federal Capital Territory had not only changed their sacrificial beasts from simple chickens, goats, sheep, and cows to humans but had also raised their charges a hundredfold. None of the big men would believe anything done for them would work if they were not charged hundreds of thousands or even millions of naira. Some medicine men had started to ask for their fees to be paid in dollars, pounds, or euros if their consultants wanted their medicines to work a hundred percent well. They would not believe anything prepared for them would work if the sacrificial beast was a mere domestic animal. To the big men, it was easier to procure a young boy or girl from the "body shop" at Sanoma Children's Home than get a live lion or leopard as some medicine men had demanded. The stakes were high and demanded equally high sacrifices and charges. Now, instead of burying huge cows for powerful medicines, the marabouts used humans who promised a higher efficacy rate of more potent medicines. Famed bishops and pastors building new national headquarters of their churches went to Sanoma Children's Home to pick their sacrificial lambs from

Mama Toko. The rousing "Praise the Lord" became more tumultuous. The same folks who contributed money to the orphanage so as to be recognized went there for their human supplies. Boys and girls were buried alive under German concrete of churches and business premises that were promised prosperity. The pastor who vied for but failed to be elected CAN President gave thanksgiving a week after he opened a new mega church that used the skull of one of the alumni of Sanoma Children's Home. Governors sought human sacrifices of virgin girls bred in the orphanage to go through the Camel's Eye in airtight cases that would have either led to conviction to life jail or impeachment.

Mabel would use her haunted mind to undermine Mama Toko's reputation. As expected, she received the sack order within three days. Mama Toko read her mind and knew that she had known too much for her comfort. It was an order and not a letter of dismissal. Mama Toko was a very smart woman and did not want to leave any paper trail in the event of a court case. She verbally dismissed Mabel and offered her seven hundred and fifty thousand naira. The director of the orphanage was surprised that the woman did not accept the money.

Mabel became "born again" in a church she was not sure did not have any link with Mama Toko's orphanage. She could not be sure because the pastors and bishops were like masquerades and you could not tell who they really were! In any case, once in the Garden of Eden Church of Christ she used her testimony to paint a gory tale of the orphanage. And that public confession was during the visit of an American evangelist in a public event televised all over the world by both CNN and Aljazeera and two Nigerian independent television stations. Mabel's testimony would lead to the collapse of the once famous Sanoma Children's Home. The chorus was expected.

"Those who rise so high must fall," some said.

"How could these things stare us in the face without being seen?" others asked.

"She's a Nigerian after all," was the headline of the *Guard*. The *Concord* ran an editorial, "Too good to be true," which in part read: "From her friends and donors, she could only be a part of the national mafia. And it was the interest of foreign children's welfare organizations, even UNICEF, and others that led to the baring of this breeding ground of children for big men and women and their medicine men for human sacrifices. We did not know that young boys and girls were also slaughtered to harvest organs—kidneys and hearts—to meet the needs of racketeers of organ parts to keep families of big folks alive. Once the wind has blown open the fowl's anus, we can now see the sorry sight. From the many men and women who came to the tribunal and torn with grief, we now know that some parents, mainly poor ones, had given out their boys and girls for adoption after being seduced with staggering amounts of money and their kids publicly taken as orphans. That mighty fence with that indomitable glittering gate of Sanoma Children's Home really covered a lot from our wide-open eyes. Thank God we are free from this satanic network that many of us had praised as a God-blessed venture."

13

MY DELTA HOME AND PEOPLE: WAFI NO DEY COME LAST

The Delta is a labyrinth of so many things, but in that maze there is a core identity. Coming to Effurun from Abuja was a sort of homecoming for me. At Abuja, despite my coming from the United States as a Nigerian, without being told, most folks knew I was from the Delta.

"Yes, na!" I had said at a drinking joint.

I had tried to pretend I was from Maiduguri but it didn't fly with my drinking mates, not just because I couldn't speak Hausa except for *kadan kadan* or Kanuri except for *kilewa sile*, but there was something in my voice and accent that was indelibly Delta. I have an inescapable accent. In the US I am foreign; in Nigeria's capital I am tagged Delta. I was spending time with folks who had paid money to watch and listen to comedians from the Delta at least once a year for so many years. They knew I had the accent of Gordons, Ali Baba, Basket Mouth, and others who had always made them laugh as they had never done in their lives before. Many have DVDs of these comedians who have established themselves as big entertainers. They are great and make a severe-faced person to laugh. If you don't laugh when they perform, then you are a depressed person that is too far gone to recover any cheerfulness. If you listen on one of Gordons' Clinics, the spirit of depression in you must be cast away until you go back home and sit alone in your house. Gordons can make a monkey, goat, or dog laugh not to talk of human beings. Gordons can make you forget your poverty or sickness at least while you are under his spell. After all, for Delta people only money and sickness can keep a person down. But you have to laugh or make others laugh to get out of the grip of your oppressors.

"Wetin man go do?"

There is something about the Delta, the so-called "core Delta," that gives its folks out. Sometime ago at Corus Hotel in central Kuala Lumpur, we were only two African-looking men in the big hotel. The other chap stared at me. I stared back for a while and turned away. When I looked towards him again, he was still staring at me. "Which kin man be this wey they look me like James Bond?" I asked myself. Before I could turn to him again, I saw him walking to me.

"Where are you from?" he asked, as he came to me.

"Nigeria by way of the United States," I told hm.

"What part of Nigeria are you from?" he asked.

"Warri," I told him.

There is the panache of many like me who introduce themselves as being from Warri but could really be from villages or smaller towns far away. After all, Warri is, if not was, the Oil City. It is the city now made popular by comedians such as Gordons, Ali Baba, Basket Mouth, I Go Die, and Away Away across Nigeria. This man must have understood that.

"You be Wafi man then?" he asked.

"Yes-o! I be real Wafi man-o!" I answered.

He embraced me tightly. He looked older than me and I greeted him "Mi guo!" We understood somehow that we were Urhobo. There is something about me, I have learnt, that gives me out as a Wafi man, a Delta man. Who knows Okpara Inland, not to talk of Okurekpo, Okurunoh, or Enemarho Village for that matter? All these places are subsumed in the glamor of Warri.

So, to Warri I came. I had come to a familiar land. I did not grow up in Warri as such but had lived there for long. So long there that I consider myself a homebody in Warri, a Wafi boy! I did my Higher School Certificate program at Federal Government College, Warri, studying English when my mates were studying popular Botany, Zoo, and Chemistry, what they endearingly called "BoZooChem." After finding my way to the University of Ibadan, I came back to teach first at Federal Government College and then at Petroleum Training Institute before the dream of an academic life took me to faraway Maiduguri. It's in Effurun that I built my first house and I call home. Effurun is Warri to us old homeboys; no matter what future politicians would do to separate Warri and Effurun; the two towns are one because they are inseparable.

There's something naughty about Warri and it shows in the entire populace or residents. The young walk with a swagger. The residual features of the *boma* boy of old, I believe. There are no more boma boys in Warri or Sapele; the last of them joined the Nigerian Army to fight against Biafra after Midwest was taken over by Biafran troops. That persisting naughty walk was the sailor's walk when Warri was in vogue with a functioning port and the sea men came to town to seek women after being starved of sex in their ships in long journeys. There were no *yansh boys* in the ships or in town then, it appears, to ease the starvation. The Warri boy moves rather slowly in a princely style. After all, his father is a king of fools. He has a roguish smile on the face which can turn sour in an instant. His mood can be likened to that of the Delta weather; now sunny and soon dark-clouded. Most times it suns while raining; a mixture of joy and pain. He is a hero and a villain in one personality. In Warri, we laugh hilariously over deep pain. The Warri boy has a magic voice; a voice that can cast a spell over others and I am not surprised that the *wayo* boys are Yahoo boys who can toast old white women in America and Canada and get away with hundreds of thousands of dollars. He can lie and be heard as telling the truth. He can misbehave outlandishly and believe that is normal. He does things the wrong way and that method often appeals to him as the right way to behave. He can drive the wrong path of the road, flashing the car light ferociously at you. He believes in intimidating the other. When you tell him to go right, he turns left because he mistrusts truth as the weapon of the weak. He does not want to be seen as weak when his genes lack strength. "Wafi no dey carry last-o!" is his battle cry. He may not be well-read but he is surely smart; very ingenious in a negative manner. He knows Machiavelli, acts like his Prince but has never heard of him or read any of such books. For how Wafi boy go read book when he fit pass with distinction without opening a book? How he go work hard and marry when he can cast a spell over any girl with his roguish smile and sugar-coated tongue? He can go and do tie-neck at any of the intersections such as Enerhen and Jakpa Junctions and make enough money to live a whole day of princely affluence. Tomorrow is another day! The Wafi boy lives the opposite of what he says he will do. When he says, "Na die I dey-o," he is doing very well. He has incorporated the character of the tortoise and Eshu into one body. It is difficult to see a grownup Warri boy. Everybody is a boy; there is no man. When he is leaving you, he says, "I dey come!" You will wait for Godot till life after death!

So, I am not surprised that when I send a boy on an errand to buy me something, he brings no change back to me. Even if you ask for the change, he acts dumb and deaf until you will embarrass yourself because of your own money and leave the burgeoning crook alone. It is a form of extortion or a coerced type of tip. The Warri boy does not wait for what you will give to him willingly; he extracts it from you. He is very proactive and believes others are slow witted. He is sharp and does things *sharp sharp*.

I decided to go for a driver's license the week after I arrived in Delta. My old license had expired. When I told Igho to accompany me to the Licensing Office, he asked me why I was going there to waste my time.

"Just give me the cash and photo and I will bring back your license later today."

"I'll like to be there myself," I explained to him.

There was chaos at the licensing office in Jakpa Road, perhaps the only one in all of Effurun. Under-age boys and girls, young and old, and some really elderly were all there, I learnt, for their driver's licenses. It stood out clearly that these folks were incapable of driving and apparently had no cars of their own. "What is going on here," I asked myself. I was facing Igho and he seemed to have read my consternation right.

"I tell you make you no come. All these ones come to get license for Western Union," he explained.

Igho had the gift of Wafi boys, that instinct to read another's mind right. I laud him for that. I wondered how these folks could get their driver's licenses without reading or road tests. Nothing at all! I was learning fast. Driver's licenses were obtained to show as IDs to collect money sent from abroad in banks.

"Na so banks dey too—full of people waiting to collect money from Western Union," Igho further explained.
I imagined the same for MoneyGram. I would learn later that there were agents for driver's licenses, car plate numbers, and other related aspects like insurance and these agents take a cut for themselves to save their real owners from wasting their time by sitting five to six hours at the mobbed Licensing Office. I discovered a very entrepreneurial talent of Nigerians to create more jobs out of nothing! Now those agents make a lot of money from folks who drive or own cars but don't have the time to waste. And so popular are the FRSC officials that one director was invited to give a keynote lecture on Chinua Achebe at a literary conference organized by a department of the University of Abuja!

Love is very practical in today's Warri. When we were young in Warri, you could take a girl to your room, sleep with her and not think of giving her money except the little amount to take a taxi back home. Some boys would even not give anything. It was not right, but the girls at that time were so trusting that they gambled with their monetary rewards. Warri girls have surely grown wiser over the decades of my absence. "Nowadays," I was lectured by one who knows, "Money for hand, back for ground." This statement was meant to communicate literarily. The boy asks the girl how much she wants and they haggle about the price before settling on a definite sum. So the amount was spelt out and she got the money from the boy before following him in a taxi or car. Money first, and then have what you desire!

I know two kinds of Warri girls or women. There are those either born or raised in Warri but do not carry the social genes now ascribed to Warri girls and those born and bred in Warri and follow what has become a social trademark trait. My wife was born and raised in Warri but she belongs to a different age and escaped the social genes of the contemporary girls. She is divine in so many ways. I have a junior colleague who is sweet and very graceful. She also belongs to the older generation, which contemporary girls will dismiss as foolish but in fact exhibit virtues that give women a lot of dignity. I also know many Warri women who do not show the traits that are now bandied as features of "Warri girls." So, though who insults women also insults his mother," as the saying goes, there are many exceptions to what has come to be branded as "Warri girls." These exceptions are some of the most gentle and affable human beings anywhere in the world. They can be selfless and patient to a fault and to them it is not just "me" but "others" most of the time. I know this fact through personal experience of close relationship with them.

However, the other type of Warri girls belongs to a class of its own. They would like to be seen or compared to Mami Wata, but they are not. They try to bleach to look fair like Mami Wata; they jerry-curl their hair and use hot combs but their hair is not Mami Wata's. They are too earthbound to be compared to a goddess, or one so alluringly beautiful, generous, and who gives out gifts and only receives compliments.

"Na sweet mouth I go chop?" they jab at you. There is something husky in their voices, a little overbearing. They want to seduce men but have learnt that these men are tortoises and troublemakers, and so have become the opposite of what they really want to be. How can a seducer be harsh, combative, aggressive, or pugnacious? You can drive your client away. No wonder love has become so banal in Warri. Their older generation watched *Love in Tokyo* in Delta and Rex Cinemas. The old generation loved romance; they loved love. Now the current generation of girls and women seem to ask themselves, "Where will love take me to in a material world?" They say love will not feed them, love will not provide them money to buy their toiletries and other needs. "Na love I go chop?" That's what they ask. And so they demand money to take care of themselves. They have not understood that friendship emanating from love could make their partners generous if they have the means. They don't believe in mutual uplifting of partners. They want money here and now!

I have an image of Warri girls and women as flippant, as if that's what the boys need to egg them on to become manly. When they speak, they shout. They don't know how to murmur into your ears. They do not understand the benefits of sweet low music. They shout. That is, unless money is involved. There is a harsh edge to their tone, but become temporarily soft-spoken when money is being passed onto their sweaty hands.

They know their parents want them married out, and woe betide the young woman without a husband. That's why they are ready to marry anybody that has the male phallus to be seen as married. They want to avoid the curse of not being married. They want to taste of the dish of marriage, sweet or sour. But marriage eludes many in the city of too many women and many men. Too many women laying ambushes for men and many men wanting to eat the baits and still not be caught in any female hooks or traps! No wonder, in Warri the women talk of "playing love."

"Make una dey play una love dey go," I heard a woman say as a couple holding hands passed by.
Of course, I was curious. I followed the woman and asked her how to play love and whether she can play love with me.

"I no cheap-o," she told me. "If you get money I fit play love with you and you go enjoy am," she said.

We both laughed.

"I go come back," I told her.

"Rat!" she said out loud and spat to the side of the road. For me, I knew I came close to a trap. But the point is that love is a game that is played all over Warri.

So, once the girls drop out of school or still in school without reading, they put their few clothes in a plastic bag and head for their boyfriends' homes to start marital life. The older men and women call it "Sapele marriage." Their shacking is also called "Township marriage."

I heard when I was visiting at Delta State University that many female students shack with male students. They live together as man and woman, husband and wife, and the female students act as housewives. When they take a motorcycle, the girl sits in front of the boy who stakes ownership over her. Often the girls suffer abuse but remain in the relationship as many of the marriages in town, I understand from those there who know what is happening. From statistics, such girls don't do well in class while the boys who already live like patriarchs do well. The girls suffer stress of housekeeping and cooking, while the boys enjoy sex and the leisure to read. I wonder what the girls gain in the relationships. Is it money or sex or both? Warri girls are strong and weak, a contradiction reconciled in their patriarchal environment. Once grownup, they are too strong as women. They are tomboys; after all they watch their brothers. But strong as they look, they are very weak. The carapace of strength is fake; a false shield. Many of them are ignorant. One of the first things I observed when I came back is the incident of so many unmarried girls, a few underage, with babies living with their parents. The girl mothers don't go to school. They go to sleep with the latest father of their youngest child late in the evening. Early in the morning they return to their parents' homes with babies strapped to their backs, often wearing jeans and T-shirts. I saw some households have two unmarried girls with two or more babies each. The parents seem paralyzed by indecision and do nothing over their daughters' condition. The irony of it is that parents of the boys, often unemployed, tolerate their sons having girlfriends still come to them in their houses to produce more babies not properly cared for. The boys and girls despite their *open eye* attitude do not yet understand that when a mature girl and boy make love, a baby is the natural result. So these princes and princesses in a hole do not know the importance of condom and other forms of contraceptives in their relationship and so Warri boys and girls breed young ones at the same exponential rate as the rats in town! Neighborhoods as Notoma in Essi Layou in Warri and Masodje in Effurun are examples, if you watch, have this phenomenon.

The Wafi girl affects sophistication in a clumsy manner. She can get away with it with outsiders but not with the homeboys. They will go now, I hear, to oil workers in Nigerian National Petroleum Corporation, Petroleum Training Institute staff, and other outsiders so many of whom live in town and want something different from where they come from. After all, Warri girls do not cover their faces. They need no cover to be themselves. They are very streetwise but intellectually empty. If you want to take her out and ask her for what she wants, she will choose the most expensive restaurant or hotel. At the restaurant she wants chicken, salad, and fried rice, their staple diet when out. At their homes they eat yam, plantain, eba, or starch. They even drink garri with beans! Outside home, they want to look sophisticated by the food and drinks they order. But you know they are preying on your lust. They want you to spend so much money to test your pocket whether you are financially resilient or not. They may pick something from one plate and the other, and then push the plates from them saying, "I don't enjoy this food." That's after you have paid a big sum for the food. They ask for shots of whiskey and lime and at parties drink bottles of Star beer without glasses. They cannot afford to buy a bottle for themselves and so, invited or not, they stampede every wedding reception and burial ceremony, to have their fill. They go with voluminous bags in which they hide drinks and fried meat they take home to testify to their attending a lavish party! They know not that they are stealing. There is no morality in their psyche. They consider their actions at parties as smart but they smack of poverty or lack of simple party etiquette. The best they take at home is Coke. And some of them have followed their street boys or street husbands to take *monkey tail*, a concoction of local gin, weed, and other intoxicants that of course inevitably leads them to bed and more babies!

Upon all the talk, they are cheap, very cheap indeed. They want to latch themselves to any man they fancy they can exploit or take care of their immediate needs. They use the word "Mugu" a lot. Yes, they celebrate each other's success with the latest mugu. To them, the mugu is the stupid man who spends recklessly for them. They think that as soon as he is dry, they will abandon him as cows do a dry waterhole. They will keep on searching for a fresh waterhole to drink and graze in a greener pasture. "Money for hand, back for ground" they adhere to shamelessly. But the mugu is not a fool. In fact, the mugu is not a *mumu* and uses his money to get what he wants without any attachment or effort. It is like outsourcing with his money. He distances the girl or woman from him and his family while getting what he wants and that's it. The girls may feel they have many boyfriends, one a schoolmate to help in assignments, a teacher to help her pass exams, a young man they really love, and a rich man they relate to for money. But the mugu makes a mumu of the girl because he can order her to come to him and she can leave her so-called true love for the mugu. Both are "mumugu" without knowing, the girl who is a gold-digger and the lusty rich man. Of course, the girls and women in Warri have no time for the *yeye* man, the useless man. Men are useless to women in Warri when they have no money. Even if impotent and with tons of money, the man is not *yeye*; he could be a real mugu!

Effurun and Warri have changed a lot. Every space along the road is crowded; if not with churches for the swarming Christians and houses for the increasing population, it is with caravans and ramshackle structures used as shops. Beside roads too are plazas, sort of shopping complexes. Thus things are sold everywhere. Many of the shoppers don't go far to buy what they sell but others travel farther than I would anticipate. I have come from Abuja and Lagos respectively in Sienna minivans with female traders coming from Dubai, India, China, and Switzerland. These are the "big-time" traders who sell wholesale or retail to other street or plaza sellers. From what I see in my Jefia Avenue area, some traders in the Plaza might not keep their shops for much longer because there isn't much patronage. Most of these traders and sellers are young women, some just from high school or others graduates. They might have gone jobless for months or years and found somebody, a rich uncle or aunt, or caught a "mugu" to set them up for the small businesses. Others have medicine stores, chemists or pharmacies, also to do retailing to make money. But since they don't go far, they get supplies locally and might be selling placebos from Aba rather than good medicines.

A few businesses seem to be popular in the Effurun-Warri axis: petrol stations, hotels, medicine stores, and private schools. In the area, once people see a small business thriving, they want to jump into it. The bandwagon effect captures my people. And so there are so many petrol stations some of which barely sell much in days unless there is fuel scarcity. Of course with greed they tamper with the pump and mix their fuel with cheaper liquids. As for hotels, there are so many that they make money only because men and women use them as joints for sexual liaisons. The schools are so many with poorly paid graduates and some teachers from the government schools that are often on strike. The gossip is that the proprietors make money by bribing exam officials to turn the other way while they bring people to help their students. In this way they perform well for the promotion of the private schools but when they enter the university many of such students are barely literate.

My nightmare in Effurun and Warri whenever I drove out were the *maruti,* the *keke.* I understand the full name is *keke na pep* got from a program in Lagos. Nigerian government officials and others import these from India which they describe as promoting entrepreneurship in the country. But it is often a way to have kickbacks in the corrupted system. These keke drivers used to be motorcycle popularly called okada drivers and drive as if there is no other person on the road. They are so greedy and impatient that, like okada drivers, they can't just wait! My car had so many brushes with keke. I had to take it for painting after many brushes. As soon as I brought it back, a keke driver in the usual hurry to pick more passengers brushed my car. He knew he was wrong.

"Oga, sir, nothing spoil for your car," he said.

"You brushed my car and you say nothing spoil?" I asked.

"Oga, I don look am, nothing spoil," he told me.

In a fit of rage, I entered my car, drove forward and aimed the back of my car at the front of his keke. I pressed it backwards and moved forward to speed away.

"Oga, you be like us before you get big man car-o," he shouted after me.

I heard but sped off. Later, I felt bad with myself. Did I really need to pay him back for denying that he spoilt my car with his keke's blue paint? I should have been more restrained. It was one of the things I did on the spur of the moment that I regretted during my stay in Effurun.

Warri evokes fond memories of the past. I decided to leave my car at the African Petroleum Station near the main motor park, also called Garage, and walk through streets I knew forty and more years earlier. Something in me pulled me to walk to Radio Road, about a half kilometer away. Yes, that was where I became immersed into the Warri spirit when living with Charles Edemenaha during holidays in my Higher School Certificate program period. Radio Road is no longer lonely. Far back in 1966/67 it was sparsely housed with an untarred road leading right from Lower Erejuwa Road. No 10, Radio Road, where we lived stood beside the Radio Station. The place is now cramped with houses. There are houses built on what should be roads, lanes, or adjoining streets. I stopped at 10 Radio Road and looked towards UCC, the United College of Commerce that we used to call "Useless College of Cassava." The builders seemed to have thrown away the street plan, if there was one at any time, and planted living structures wherever they found space. I shook my head at how ugly things had become. The new inhabitants of 10 Radio Road were out because the doors were locked. I turned to go back to explore some other parts of the Warri I knew.

I passed Sam Warri Essi Road, entered Enemejuwa, to retrace Okoye Street. The two earlier streets have not changed all the years. Of course, they have become more crowded. The roads must have been tarred so many years back and cars parked on both sides of the road. Ahead was Okoye Street that evoked memories of youth. Okoye Street is there without the folks that made it so well known for good or bad. It has lost its notoriety. That used to be the warehouse of prostitutes for decades. Even though passing through there reduced my trip to the Post Office and the market in those days, I avoided it when young because whoever passed through there was suspected rightly or wrongly of seeking the women there. Once they saw you, they would beckon on you to come to them.

"Come make I teach you love," some would say, if they knew you were very young.

"Come make I give you honey love," others would say.

They used different slogans to invite male passersby to stop at their rooms for sex. It was the days before AIDS but still many men would have contracted other types of STDs, especially gonorrhea and syphilis. It appears the houses have long been repainted after the *ashewo* inhabitants left the place. It has lost its weird smell that used to make me feel like throwing up after going through the street. Was that smell of sex or my mind assaulted by the odor of imagined sex?

I passed there to Ginuwa, then Igbi Street, and through Mowoe Road to the Post Office. For me the walking was reliving old days but the place has changed. It has so changed that it has remained more haggard than it used to be. I had stopped at Robert Road and the pharmacy was still there, far more vibrant now than ever.

"Do you have Cipro?" I asked because my stock had run out and I needed to have some ready just in case I had stomachache.

"What is wrong with you?" the lady asked.

I realized that I was in Warri where people answered questions with questions.

"Do you have Cipro or not?" I asked again.

"No be you I dey ask wetin dey pain you?" she said,
as if I would understand Pidgin better.

"Is this a pharmacy or a clinic?" I asked.

"Where you come from to dey ask that question?"

Many people who came to buy medicines were
staring at us and must have been surprised that I was
exchanging questions with the chemist.

"Must you know where I come from to sell me
medicine?"

"Why did you come here if you don't want to buy
medicine?"

"Are you a doctor or seller of medicine?"

"E don do for una!" one of the men waiting shouted.

"Who be this too-know man self?" another asked.

I carefully withdrew and entered Robert Road to take
a keke back to my car parked at the African Petroleum station
near the Garage.

* * *

I travelled in the Niger Delta and put the account of
my journey in verse.

Datelines

1. Nembe

It's not the end of the world as imagined far from here
though the waterways defy mapping by outsiders; the boat
wriggles through labyrinths of creeks at high tide steering
to the island city; the same facility as footways in the forest.
The water, muddy brine, does not invite for leg and face wash
and I miss a necessary water ritual I am so used to
performing—
the fishless waterscape and bird-less airspace dissuade me
from embracing invisible water spirits that thronged therein.

It started raining on the open speed boat while midway from Ogbia
and tarpaulin spread to cover heads; we were human cargoes in
the boat that bounced hard on and off waves at its light tail-end
in the chilly breeze of a cheerless landscape; an adventure ahead.
The pilot stood at the helm, a veteran boatman of waterways
to whom the thousands of creeks hold no mysteries or fear
and directed the boat from water hyacinths and wide deep waters
choosing to steer by the river's edge, perhaps in anticipation of
a wreck and we clutching to stilted mangrove roots for life's sake.
We bounced up and down absorbing the cool desolate air
now at water crossroads, then at creeks and wider deep waters
flowing majestically but dour from afflictions of oil and fumes.

From one Nembe village to another, passing fishing villages,
the destination soon in sight—from afar a sentinel town
guarding big and small creeks for warriors that made it a power.
To enter town the boatman must pass through three different
military posts—the first unfocussed passed us waving; at the next
post a soldier barked at our host's friend "Remove your specs!"
which she did instantly because nobody wanted trouble for a vacation.
And soon we docked at the very gate of our host's compound,
a villa set elegantly on a refilled mangrove swamp overlooking a river.
"Welcome to Nembe!" he tells us, and I am not at the world's end

but a devastated land struggling to live modern despite all
odds.

2. Brass

Even a bigger exile island than Amassoma is Brass
in its trinity of Twon Brass, Ewama, and Okpoama.
There are cars here and the ancient has ceded to new
realities an abundance. "Brass is prosperous," says
my guide, who heads the motorcycle riders' association.
Of Brass's age, nobody disputes the age of this turtle
with the patchwork of centuries inscribed everywhere.
"That was the colonial headquarters," my guide points,
as he rides to show the divided cemetery of blacks
and whites, the absurdity of brittle bones and rot.
At the open mouth of the Atlantic, it was inevitable
for the Portuguese first, then the British, to enter town.

But Brass embraces all shades of humanity and faith
in the potentials of all; hence forebears of so-called
witches take pride, after rejection in their home clans,
in the high fortune of sons and daughters whose
great-grand-mothers bore to Ijo fathers. They have
legitimate foothold in undiscriminating Brass—
the current local government chairman a descendant;
here and there the guide points to Urhobo-descended
medical doctors, businessmen, and politicians; diaspora
population that has outperformed their homeland's.

At Ewama a new town under construction by the State
after two brothers heading each side of town fought
such a senseless war not only killing themselves but
also abandoning the town for good; no victor, no
vanquished. And yet all will soon be victors in mansions
as the state government completes story buildings

to bring back refugee fighters who fled their ghosts.
Reconciliation Brass style, compensation Bayelsa style!

At Okpoama the Atlantic stares at you from infinity,
a beach stretching beyond Myrtle Beach or Montego Bay
that only hosts parties at Easter and Christmas holidays;
what should be a year-round vacation oceanfront view.
The guide rode me along the beach sand for kilometers
farther south to where the ocean is devouring land
without looking back spiting those rich but foolish enough
to build their refuge homes outside ramshackle capitals.
One of such told about the sea's inevitability retorts:
"If I can use the house for ten years, that will be enough,"
and that for a 100 million-naira villa to which
he comes with his children once a year to fish!

There's original *tombo* wine but no crops grow here;
everything from garri, yam, to tomato imported—"Nothing
grows here because of the pollution," the guide tells me.
The Amayanebo, a former governor, lives in Port Harcourt
far from the court he presides over and far from his people.
Another rich man is waiting in line to mount the throne;
neither primogeniture nor royal houses; free enterprise.

Agip supplies light free to all residents of Brass;
the roads concrete slabs that will outlive decades.
Then I head for the famous fish pepper soup joint
not to lose the details for which Brass brought me;
after which I buy ground periwinkles and a barracuda.
Twon Brass is both my entry and departure points.
And the waiting boatman helps us in and to Ogbia,
gateway to inland life, he steers atop ocean waves
through trademark labyrinths of oil-soaked creeks.

- Brass Island is made up of three adjoining towns: Twon Brass, Ewama, and Okpoama.
- Nembe: an island town in Nigeria's Bayelsa State; a major oil industry center.

14

CAN'T WAIT!

(I found Warri interesting and wrote this story on my experience there.)

The motorcycle was always the culprit. For the inordinate greed that led to speeding on a narrow rugged road. It was guilty of robbery; it was equally guilty of violence. Whatever dastardly act done, the motorcycle always came out condemned. The verdict had always been the same: Guilty! It farted along the way. It coughed without stop and did not cover its mouth exhaling stale breath. It smoked furiously. Its fumes did not bother its rider. People used to smoking cigarettes and inhaling fumes of Bell Oil Company's gas flares beside their farms and homes took the acrid smoke as another flavor in their now acquired voluntary and involuntary smoking habits.

The motorcycle, a neglected assistant, was not adequately maintained. Beauty has to be maintained to remain beautiful, the saying goes. The rider stretched the motorcycle's patience hour to hour, day to day, week to week, and month to month. It was a rare feat for one to live beyond a year with all the hazards that it had to go through. The indefatigable rider believed the iron mule would always trot along when whipped with a starter. Once there was fuel in the stomach, it would move. It was a living miracle that would continue to run with or without rest as long as it was filled with fuel.

"Tomorrow, when I make three thousand naira, I'll take it to the mechanic."

The following day, like one that could be exploited without protest, its driver broke the promise without qualms.

"Machine no be man! E fit work every day without rest. Not me dey ride am? If I no tire, how e go tire?"

That day the rider made four thousand naira, and that made him daydream about buying another motorbike to give out for rent. Good business is a soap that foams and foams when used in washing. The motorbike business was a good one. Of course, if the motorcycle increased his earnings that day, it could go on for one more day or a few more days before the weekend.

"Man dey wait for weeks and months to get what e want, why can't okada wait a few more days before mechanic fix am well well?" the rider asked.

It was not clear whether he was asking himself or the okada, who must have fallen deaf for all the revving that went on in the name of speed. Of course, the motorcycle had to wait till the iron mule driver was ready to part with a fraction of the money it made for him. Exploitation has always been there for the helpless, and the okada bore its aches but still cranked on when started. It did not have the voice to say "God dey!" as humans in its position would have done. It did not have the capacity for peaceful or non-violent protests until it broke down.

The motorcycle was found guilty of impatience that led to the death of a pedestrian at a boldly marked zebra crossing. Really it was manslaughter. Only the motorcycle was found guilty. Neither the rider who sped along as if pursued nor the passenger standing where he should not was culpable. It spent time in the police station until the rider paid for its release. Twenty minutes before another accident, a passenger had coaxed the driver on to the disaster.

"I am already late. I want to be there in no time."

"Don't worry," the driver had assured, as the passenger placed the crispy one hundred naira note on his right palm.

He had started the engine with a flourish. Even a stunt man would not have done better. With one leg stretched backwards, his behind in the air, his right hand revved the engine with a stuttering staccato that belched out smoke that heralded the mad race to his destination. The motorcycle, not the driver, flew through the snail-paced snaking traffic. It veered north, east, between cars, almost knocking down whatever was on its path. And then *gbaaam*! Bystanders and passersby gasped at the extent of the devastation. So much speed through a walking zone. The motorcycle had claimed another victim. It knocked down a pedestrian, who hemorrhaged to death before any assistance could come. It would take one hour to reach the hospital for an ambulance and there would be no fuel to drive it. Of course, the person knocked down bled and bled before onlookers, and gave up life.

Even a cat of seven lives would not have escaped the impact of the flying heavy metal of a motorcycle upon the man walking. The police had arrived soon to start the investigation that would lead to prosecution. Things usually went one way—the culprit rider would bribe the police with his year's salary and the case would go nowhere. "After all, the deceased was closing his eyes and stood on the road where cars and motorcycles pass," the barely readable police report concluded. Case closed! The motorcycle rider breathed a sigh of relief and the following day, the rider got his motorbike back from police custody and gave it a bath that rid it of human blood stains. Immediately the bath was over, the rider put his clean iron mule to service again.

*　　*　　*

Another day there was another memorable but unpleasant experience. The motorcycle was rude, crude, and obscene.

"You dey craze?" the rider shouted.

"Na your mama dey craze!" was the swift response.

"You be ashewo!"

"Na your wife be ashewo!"

At the destination, another harangue began.

"No be hundred naira we talk?"

"I no go take only one hundred naira. The distance pass this money. Bring another thirty naira."

"Na only the hundred naira I don give you I get."

"You go pay me today or you no dey go anywhere."

"Make I see how you go hold me for here."

The scuffle that ensued went on till both realized the wasted effort and went their separate ways. It was the motorcycle that caused the argument and not the attitudes of the driver and the passenger.

*　*　*

One regular day as the driver scrambled on the busy street, the motorcycle screeched to a noisy halt. It howled a dying groan before it fell silent. The driver tried to re-start the engine but it would not start. Checking the engine, there was no oil. The motorcycle's heart had failed. The rider did not weep for the okada; he wept for the loss of naira he would have made the rest of that day and the following days. He needed the iron mule to come back to life to complete his own life. Tomorrow it would go to the mechanic and stay in the workshop for a week. There the mechanic would perform his miracle. The mechanic performed surgery on the failed heart of iron that would make the okada be on its feet and racing again. Wonder of wonders! Only the motorcycle died and resurrected in the land. The mechanic was the miracle worker whose touch and attention would bring the dead back to life.

*　*　*

Only an okada man would lose his leg and not know and still go on as if nothing had happened to him. The leg tore off his body after the collision with a car, but the motorcyclist rode on. Onlookers, who had screamed in shock at the ghastly accident, stared at him as he rode away. They wondered how one could go on that way—legless and still riding a motorcycle, without any indication of the torn-off ligaments and leg and the bleeding that followed. Fortunately, there was no passenger. The okada rider was racing to pick a teacher from Ekpan Elementary School, a few kilometers away. He wanted to get that done as soon as possible so as to go to his favorite street to make more money that afternoon. The car owner had, on his part, sustained severe injuries too and came down to inspect his car and stretch his neck. He had jerked forward to knock his head against the dashboard; he was not wearing his seat belt.

At Jakpa Junction, the crowd of cyclists, motorists, pedestrians, and hawkers of articles brought movement to a halt. There was no way the stunt rider would fly over them because he would still land on people! Then Tefe was compelled to slow down and, as he mentally used his leg to press the gear, he physically felt the wound and bleeding. He had no right foot to press down the lever of the gear. The pain stung him instantly and he fell clumsily from the roaring but disabled machine.

Fellow motorcyclists noticed the emergency at hand. They belonged to an association and took each other as a brother. In fact, others saw them as if they were members of a cult or a fraternity in the way they took the other's problem as theirs and communicated with secret signs. Those who saw the extent of the wound were aghast at the savagery of the crude amputation. They took him up and set him on another motorcycle's passenger seat and took off for the nearest clinic around. Tefe sat behind the motorcyclist, while somebody else sat behind him so as to steady him on the seat.

The rider revved the engine, which exhaled thick dark fumes and acrid breath. Belonging to the same secret society, the riders had mastered the same craft. In a matter of seconds, this rescue iron mule was meandering swiftly through heavy traffic as the amputee wailed sharply from intensifying pain and bleeding. It was as if he had been sleeping before now or the leg had been numbed and the alleviating medicine had worn out. The pain was sharp and biting—needles were piercing the raw flesh with vengeance.

Miraculously, another motorcyclist arrived at the same time at Castle Clinic with the severed leg. He must have come by air through the crammed streets. Ovie Palace Road, where the clinic stood, was swarmed with onlookers amazed at what they were seeing. In Effurun, people gathered where there was a free spectacle, and this severed leg was one such treat. Children, women, and men swarmed to the gate of the clinic to see what was happening. Many would not see anything but hear bits of news that they would embellish and relay to others who could not see things firsthand.

Tefe did not see his other leg that had been cut off before the doctor and his team of nurses knocked him out with anesthesia. He did not know how for hours his leg was sewed back to his hip. Yes, sewed back to his hip, as if he had lost nothing. His first response to what had happened after he regained consciousness and the pain kept at bay with strong morpheme injection was asking the nurse, "My okada well?" like one asking of a darling partner after an accident. And that was despite treating it like a slave before now, the same way a patriarchal man treated his hardworking wife until she was not around.

"You go ask your brothers who brought you here."

"Make them no thief my machine-o!"

"You bring am here?" the nurse asked.

"No be him bring me here?" he asked.

The nurse could only shake her head. Now she realized what she had heard was true—the motorcycle and its rider had the same personality. In addition to the morpheme, the doctor prescribed Codeine to ease the pain.

*　　　*　　　*

After staying in the clinic for three weeks, Tefe was discharged to return home. He would stay at home for a year, longer than the average lifespan of an okada, and spend all the money he had gained in five years of killing different okadas in paying his medical bills. At least one iron mule had taken its revenge. As Tefe recovered, he did not want anything to do with the motorcycle again. He preferred to walk with a limp than take okada to anywhere. And he would not ride any!

15

SECURITY, IKOGOSI RESORT, AND THE LAST DAYS AT HOME

I was in Johannesburg, South Africa, when two significant happenings that exposed the state of security in Nigeria took place. There were the Nyanya bus station bombings and the kidnaping of the Chibok high school girls. Both incidents have been attributed to the Boko Haram Islamist terrorist group. Yes, these two events caught the attention of the nation and the entire world. I had calls from the United States when I arrived back in Nigeria asking about my safety.

"Are you safe there in Nigeria?" one called.

"Yes, I am. Warri is far from Nyanya. In fact, Nyanya is not Abuja and I will be going back there soon," I replied.

"Keep safe!"

"Thanks."

I knew I had to keep safe. Interestingly, I used to receive calls from Nigeria when in Charlotte to be safe. That is when there were police shootings in the United States. The folks in Nigeria who called me felt that whatever happened in one part of the United States affected me irrespective of where I lived.

"That place must be a jungle," some would tell me.

"No, it's very safe. However, it depends on where you are," I would explain.

"Be careful over there," the advice would come from thousands of miles away across the Atlantic Ocean.

Nigeria is very unsafe and that is not because of only the bombing of the bus station and the kidnaping of the Chibok school girls and other women from the area. The indiscriminate violence unleashed by Boko Haram that the world hears so much about is only a fraction though significant of the daily insecurity in Nigeria. Anytime one travels in Nigeria, one is facing insecurity. Pastors out there without a church or congregation hustle for money by staying at "garages," "motor parks," bus stations, and other transport stations to pray before any filled vehicle takes off. At the end of the prayers, they ask for "offerings" by stretching out their hands and many of the passengers tip them with whatever amount they wish. But the prayer from these men of god and the "offerings" are no insurance against numerous accidents on Nigerian roads.

The roads are death traps and accidents occur so often in the potholed ill-maintained roads. Many drivers are brainless and drive without concern for other drivers and the safety of their passengers. The bus drivers drink Stout beer to keep them awake but that mars their concentration. In fact, one is more likely to die in a road accident in Nigeria than any disease or violent act of Boko Haram! Air travel is also insecure as planes tend not to be well maintained. Many observers believe that the owners of the airlines often bribe the inspectors to "pass" their dilapidated planes as air-worthy when they are not. I am surprised the men of god have not started to go to airports to pray, as they do at taxi and bus stations, before take-off. On the road there are armed robbers that waylay travelers. And there are other nefarious people on the roads night and day. Armed robbers can break into your house at night. When somebody asks one to be safe in Nigeria, how safe can one really be?

It came as a rude awakening. It was a shock that I least imagined would befall me. Until something you hear from afar happens so close to you, you never really know the impact. One begins to even believe that what happens so far away would never come close or to oneself. That's the way life goes. It has to happen to you or come very close before you are really shaken from the false sense of security that a practical mind should know always lurks around. One morning call to Peter whose play and poems I have been reading to discuss my impression of his work and the rude awakening came. I pressed his name that is programmed with his number and his phone started with the music indicating the phone is ringing. Nigerian phones, the only ones I know of in the entire world, do not just ring. Rather they play music, a jingle, and some even have excerpts of the Bible read. The owner of the phone compels you to listen to something he or she likes and perhaps defines him or her before answering you. Peter's ringing tune is simple pop music which I enjoyed but whose artiste I don't know. He picked the call. On normal times, as I know him, he would greet me and we would go through the courtesies of how our families are faring. But this time, none of such. Boom, came the punch.

"Sir, have you heard that Mrs. Ojaruega was kidnaped?"

Of course, both of them, Peter and Enajite, and other writers and scholars had come to my house for my New Year annual social gathering in my house in Effurun on January 2 whenever I spend that time in the Delta. The last one had been most interesting and lively from the discussion that went on as we ate and drank in-between discussions of encouraging young writers and scholars on how best they could position themselves for the future to succeed.

"Whaaat!" I screamed out loud.

Luckily I lived alone. If I did not, that my scream could have caused someone else a heart attack. If I were outside, my scream would have turned all eyes on me. I was alone, just after breakfast and ready for the day's tasks as marked on my calendar.

"They kidnaped her yesterday morning," he told me.

I felt betrayed by those I knew at the University who should inform me should something of this sort happen. They didn't. Twenty-four hours later they had not cared to call me. For me to know a whole day after the fact made me look so insignificant and isolated at the same time. At Effurun I did not keep company in the sense of receiving visitors. Only Dr. Jonathan came from Sapele and I occasionally drove to Sapele to see him. But there was no one there in Effurun, Warri, or Abraka who came to me. I deliberately wanted to keep a low profile so as to be invisible in the land of spirits. However, I talked on the phone and, being in the same department and discipline, I expected to have been contacted about what had befallen a junior colleague. I took it that I did not belong here as sometimes I did not belong in Charlotte. How could both Sunny and Karoh of all people not find it necessary to inform me of the kidnaping or check whether I heard or not? I am not one of them; not taken as a member of the "family" much as I tried to insert myself.

I think Peter would have found me rude because I was so confused that I dropped the call. This kidnaping could have happened to me. Yes, it could have been me kidnaped as I drove through the same stretch of road with my 4-Runner to and from Abraka. If someone driving a small car could be kidnaped, what of one driving a jeep that conjures up images of wealth in the minds of Niger Deltans? To them any jeep is a rich man's car. And it did not matter whether it was a used car; mine a 2002 model. If a junior local academic could be kidnaped, what would happen to a senior academic from the United States? I had taken too much for granted in driving without attention to security when all around me were kidnapers, armed robbers, and a pack of killers and extortionists on the loose.

I called Karoh, Enajite's best friend from my observation, whom I had known from my Maiduguri days since her father was my friend.

"Why didn't you inform me when you heard that your friend had been abducted?"

"Sir, I tried but couldn't reach you," she said.

The lie was palpable. She should have told me that it did not come to her mind that she should have informed me. But I didn't blame her because she would have been jolted as I was when she heard and so would have been so confused that thought of a visiting senior colleague would not have come to her as a person to inform about the bad news.

I called Sunny.

"Sir, I called but the network was bad," he said.

The network was to blame for his forgetfulness. Again, it was just that I expected him to call me because we were close and he should inform me about what happened in the Department. In any case, you don't just call once and give up when there's an emergency. Neither Karoh nor Sunny felt I was close enough to persist in calling me.

"Where was she kidnaped?" I asked.

"At the outskirts of Eku," Sunny told me.

I dropped the phone and in a moment knew that was so close to my Okurekpo, only three miles from Eku whose outskirts should be in our backyard. There is nowhere else to take a kidnaped victim to on that road other than to go back through the Okpara Inland-Okpara Waterside Road. And then, no kidnaper was going to go to Okpara Inland or Okpara Waterside. The kidnapers had to make a detour somewhere they could hide in. My instant realization was that they had to take a pliable bush road and there was none other than the one to Kokori villages. I called Ohwode who lives in my father's house at Enemarho Village.

"They kidnaped one of our Abraka lecturers yesterday," I told him.

"Is the kidnaped person a woman?" he asked.

"Yes," I said.

"Then they took her through here yesterday late morning."

"Did you see her?" I asked.

"No, but they took a woman through here yesterday and they must have gone to Ekraka or any nearby village," he further explained.

"Thank you so much. Please check and forward to me any lead. The kidnaped woman is my junior colleague at Abraka."

How will I not be angry that I didn't hear about the kidnaping early enough? If I had heard of it, we might have tracked the kidnapers to their den or wherever they took her when they were not yet settled. I had heard that often the kidnapers on the road and those who keep the victim hostage may not be the same group. Even among criminals, each to his task!

I called Sunny to pass the information to him.

"Call the Secret Service and the Anti-Kidnaping Director and pass them the information. I will text you their numbers," he told me.

He texted me the two numbers and I would pass the information to them to check the Ekraka area.

"Yes," the anti-kidnaping chief told me. "That's the area we are suspecting too and we will focus on that area for the search and rescue."

Enajite would be released after ten days, after the kidnapers must have satisfied themselves that they had reason to give her up. Ten days in the elements and only freed after her kidnapers had put a ransom on her head. Ten days that would destroy a weak person. She came out strong and from the streams she waded through neck-deep and the exposure to rain and sun, and being moved over four times, I shivered at how I would have fared under those harsh circumstances. I might have survived but who knows I could have buckled. I might have been the victim and the thought of being kidnaped began to haunt me. That haunting feeling would occupy me for the remaining weeks of my fellowship that I spent in Effurun.

I would imprison myself for fear of kidnapers. I stayed at home almost all day. When I went out, it had to be in broad daylight. But who told me that kidnapers don't work during the day? That in fact was when they worked the most. They saw clearly whom they wanted to abduct. They were not paid assassins who knew you and could lurk in the dark to kill for as low as 100,000 naira! Those who extort millions of naira as ransom through kidnaping did not hide and so choose to operate whenever they wish they could easily abduct their victims. But I had to leave home for one thing or another. I had to eat. I had to stretch myself. I had to get fuel for my generator, if not for my car. I could not send other people to do everything for me. I wore T-shirt most of the time. Sometimes I wore jeans or regular trousers. I would suspect every young man or woman I met as a potential kidnaper or one who would sell me out. Either they would carry out the operation or inform others to do the dastardly act.

I could not hide, much as I thought I was doing so. Or I was a swimmer whose back betrayed my underwater immersion. The month of May is in the raining season and it rains heavily in Effurun and Warri at this time. The weather is often unpredictable and there are no radio or television weather forecasts to forewarn you of bad weather. One takes things as they come. I drove only five minutes or so to pick wheat bread from Agofure Supermarket opposite the Petroleum Training Institute. A heavy downpour deluged the streets. On my return home as I branched into Ubuara Close, I fell into a gutter. The more I revved the engine to give it power to accelerate and force me out of the gutter, the more I went in. The rain had stopped as unpredictably as it had started. Soon young men gathered. They could not push the car out of the gutter—the jeep had automatic transmission and so could not be pushed no matter the number of hands. There were suggestions from many of the young men that were tried to bring out the car but all to no avail. Later planks were brought and laid on the ground through which the car later rolled through. I thanked the young men who came out to assist me. I gave them two thousand naira to treat themselves to drinks. They had all been good Samaritans to me.

"Prof, you stayed long this time-o," one of the young men told me.

I was taken aback because I didn't know him and yet he seemed to know me very well. How did he know that I am a professor? What I had thought to be self-effacing behavior did not cover the fact that I was a professor.

"I have a brother in America who does not come home," another told me.

So this fellow knew I was from America.

"Always curve to the left when turning into All Saints Street. I always see you veer too far to the right every time you are passing," another said.

He lived in the first house to the left as one entered Ubuara Close from All Saints Road and knew that I drove out every morning at about six o'clock, he told me. I was being monitored without my knowing. I was very exposed while thinking all along that I was invisible.

"God save me!" I intoned internally.

The following morning, somebody came to see me from Bayelsa and, according to him, the first person he asked about my residence as he entered the street directed him to where I lived! I was an ostrich whose head was deep in the sand but quite visible to everybody. Any hunter could easily have knocked me down!

I could not live like this, in self-incarceration. There should be another way of living. Yes, I am free at Abuja but that's not a place for writers. It is not a place for me. It is sterile and corrupting. If I could not stay in Effurun/Warri safely, I have had enough of home. I have many homes and I prepared to go to another home where I can exercise some degree of freedom without fear of kidnapers, armed robbers, witches, and spiritual attackers. There is the land of the brave. There are too many guns there too, I realized. Nowhere is safe as such but there I feel safer. But I still had two weeks before leaving for Charlotte to be with my family. I thought of where to go to let myself go before leaving the land of spirits. I thought of Obudu Ranch. It was too far to get to. I thought of Badagry but was not sure of what to find there. Yes, there's the Ikogosi Warm and Cold Springs Resort. Let me seek refuge there.

I chartered a taxi from the Effurun Motor Park to take me directly to Ikogosi. Many of the drivers had heard of Ikogosi but had not been there. They passed the bold sign leading to Ikogosi in Ekiti State as they ply the roads from Effurun through Edo and Ondo States to Ilorin in Kwara State.

"Oga e far-o," one driver told me.
"E no far reach Ilorin," I said.
"How much you go pay?" he asked.
"How much you go take?" I asked back.
In Warri and Effurun, you respond to a question with a question.
"Forty thousand go do?" he asked.
"Na Kano or Sokoro I dey go? Twenty thousand no do?" I asked back.
"You go buy fuel?"
"You go reduce the money I wan pay you?"
We settled on twenty-five thousand plus my paying to fuel the car. I asked him if I could pay double for him to come back the day I would leave there to bring me back to Effurun. He agreed. Apparently, he struck a good bargain. I knew I would buy food for him on the way and take good care of him to drive carefully. I also felt good about the bargain.
I had heard of Ikogosi since my undergraduate school days at the University of Ibadan but I had no idea of where it

was. I had read in newspapers about its warm and cold springs and the suggestion for it to be developed into a tourist resort. I had placed it far beyond where it really is—in Ekiti State. Ironically, the promotion on the web or in papers directs folks through Akure and one would think Ikogosi is located in Ondo State but it is not. Yes, Ikogosi is in Ekiti State but not far from Akure. I had been to Akure many times, the last time before this was to participate in the Association of Nigerian Authors' annual convention there some five months earlier. So, I had no problem taking the Warri-Benin Road and at Oluku Junction we branched into the road leading through Agbanikaka, Owo, to Akure and then turn right to Ikogosi. I looked out for Agbanikaka, where long ago before the Ore-Lagos Road opened we took to Ibadan in my undergraduate days. Agbanikaka is still there but has lost its glamor. It has gone down since the opening of the Ore Road and motorists took the more direct route to Ibadan and Lagos. The crowd of drivers and passengers stopping to eat at Agbanikaka ceased when that road was deserted. It lost its place as a rest station for eating and buying gifts to take home, as well as the commotion of camaraderie of travelers. We drove past Ogbese, where a traditional Warri Province ruler was exiled to in the 1960s. And then we reached Owo, that town or kingdom that stood between Ife and Benin and whose art was a blending of the two. Owo mediated between the two classic African art traditions and I am still at a loss sometimes to tell whether Owo is Ife or Benin. Owo is still Owo with an educated traditional ruler and a large polytechnic.

At Akure the driver and I stopped to eat and rest before taking off on the road leading to Ilorin. We passed the Federal University of Akure. I remembered that one of my colleagues at Federal Government College, Warri, Jerry, was a Professor there. Jerry had married a former student of our college and both had been there. I have heard many good things about the university despite the poor climate of education in the country.

I think it had been rated high among African universities not too long ago. Not too far on that road we turned right on our way to Ikogosi. We had to make more turns to the left until we arrived at the small town. There I bought recharge cards for my phones but that was not my destination. The resort was further down the road.

Ikogosi impressed me by its serenity, maintenance, and overall greenery. I have been to Bellagio, Italy, twice. I have been to Valparaiso in the Almeria region of Southern Spain, been to Hawthornden Castle near Edinburgh in Scotland, been to many islands in the Caribbean, been in Colombia and South Africa, and have loved those places. However, Ikogosi is a wonder that gladdens my heart. We have this and one does not need to travel to a far country to enjoy the peace, beauty, and blessings of nature. As our people say, one does not need to travel to the city of Sokoto when what one wants is in one's *sokoto*, one's own gown's pockets! You drive for miles and miles into the wilds until it reveals itself serenely and perching expansively from the foot to the top of a hill. Its lush tropical forest and streams take your breath away. This is a tropical paradise.

The resort has accommodation for over a hundred people but when I checked in, I did not see any other person around. Now and then a few people would come but very few took rooms to pass the night. Rather, people came in and left the same day. Oftentimes students came on excursion from as far as Lagos and Ibadan but very few spent nights there. Some locals from Ado Ekiti came to drink, eat, or swim and were off by late evening.

The complex was manicured; lawns mowed down and green with luxuriance. The roads were tarred smooth and there were carts to drive one to any part of the resort, if one does not want to explore the terrain on foot. The officials were very courteous; perhaps the best professionally trained workers I have ever come across in Nigeria. I think Governor Fayemi spent a lot of money to build and maintain the structures and train the workers. It is very well landscaped. Walking from my room to the springs was a twice daily pilgrimage. I went by the amphitheater on a wooden bridge over marshlands with different types of trees over brooks of warm water that flowed perennially. You pass by the swimming pool of warm spring water, the healthiest pool you can ever imagine—natural warm water and no chlorine! I would revive my swimming interest and dip into the pool morning and evening when I was there.

I went as many times as possible to the meeting point of the warm and cold springs, both flowing from uphill downhill. The source of the warm springs is not far away; you take staggered steps up and within five minutes you are there with pools of warm water. You cannot go beyond there but many just stop to stay and drink from the warm springs. Folks come from the town to fetch water from the springs which has medicinal qualities, they say. I drank the spring water rather than bottled water most of the time I was there. To the right coming down in a winding manner is the cold spring brook. There is a plaque marking the meeting point of the two springs. It is incredible that the stream flowing southwards has for a short distance warm water to the right and cold water to the left at the same time. The cold and the warm parallel undercurrents merge into a lukewarm flow.

I would ask questions about what lay beyond where we were allowed to reach. Was it a mystical place where the ancestors had shrines? There must be something there that the ancestors would have known that bars folks from going beyond there. The thick forest covers the lush place and there are trees and birds I saw as a child in my Ibada Village bush that I had not seen for over forty-five years that I saw there. There were firs, bread fruit trees, and other trees that populate wetlands. It is an eco-friendly resort that offers the peace and the soothing atmosphere of an Edenic existence. By the time I left Ikogosi, I had absorbed a kind of peace beyond understanding.

My safe stay at home that was another home deserved thanksgiving. If I were still a homeboy, I would have organized a big thanksgiving church service and party afterwards. I would have given my pastor a date so that it would be in the bulletin for people to look forward to for the America-based Professor to fete his people. I anticipate such services and parties to have in attendance potential kidnapers, armed robbers, witches and other "attackers." Lord, let this pass me by," I prayed. "You know I am forever and always grateful for your protection." I needed no man of god to tell me how to thank the Almighty.

As I entered the plane, after the boarding announcement was made, I gave a sigh of relief. At last, I am leaving home for home. I realized that I was forever destined to leave one home for another and the leaving and returning would stop with the one year in the land of spirits.

Printed in the United States
By Bookmasters